THE VENTURE CAPITAL ALTERNATIVE

THE VENTURE CAPITAL ALTERNATIVE

A BLUEPRINT FOR A *BETTER* PATENT SYSTEM

MATT MOYERS

COPYRIGHT © 2026 MATT MOYERS

THE VENTURE CAPITAL ALTERNATIVE
A Blueprint for a Better Patent System

FIRST EDITION

ISBN   978-1-5445-5102-9   *Hardcover*
       978-1-5445-5101-2   *Paperback*
       978-1-5445-5103-6   *Ebook*

www.thevcalternative.com

For Jack and Josie;

inventors and creators; and

regulators, politicians, auditors, judges, IP attorneys, investors, founders, C-suites, boards of directors, teachers, financial analysts, entrepreneurs, capitalists, and the United States Patent and Trademark Office.

CONTENTS

PREFACE 9

SECTION 1: RAY YARRIS AND TECHNOLOGY, IP, AND PATENT VALUATION

1. HOW FINANCE EXPLAINS THE BROKEN US PATENT SYSTEM..15
2. THE IP PYRAMID FORTRESS 31
3. THE PATENT WARS NEVER ENDED 53
4. REDISCOVERING IP CAPITAL 77
5. TIMING IS EVERYTHING......103

SECTION 2: SATOSHI NODA AND PATENT STRATEGIES

6. DISRUPTING CREDIT CARDS......119
7. INVESTOR HELL......129
8. EVOLVING PATENT STRATEGIES 147
9. THE DOUBLE-EDGED SWORD OF IP ATTORNEYS......169

SECTION 3: FIXING THE PATENT SYSTEM

10. THE GOVERNMENT'S ROLE IN FIXING PATENTS......185
11. REBUILD THE SYSTEM......205
12. BUILDING AND PAYING FOR THE NEW PATENT SYSTEM......217

ACKNOWLEDGMENTS 229
GLOSSARY......231
REFERENCES......237

PREFACE

Writing a book about patents and intellectual property (IP) valuation first came into my mind in the fall of 2013. I was working on the two largest IP valuation cases of my life, and it was not easy. Two multibillion-dollar companies, Nortel Networks and Cengage Publishing, had declared bankruptcy, and my team was called in to value the IP during the administration process.

Corporate bankruptcy is a wild process, and the bigger the default, the more contentious the investors who are losing their investment. Cengage was doing a restructuring, and its copyrights were subject to intense scrutiny because the debt lender had not properly secured all copyrights as debt collateral. My team was tasked with valuing copyrights without a security interest lien, which was about forty thousand copyright titles out of a library of hundreds of thousands of copyrights.

Nortel Networks was an even bigger issue because it was in Chapter 7 liquidation, meaning that the company's operations were being completely wound down. Everything was being sold, including the patent portfolio of nearly 3,600 patents. The liquidation administrators had managed to do the unthinkable when they sold Nortel's patents through a stalking-horse auction process that netted a winning bid of $4.5 billion, over fourteen times higher than the initial bid of $314 million. With the price of Nortel's patent portfolio settled through the auction process, the task of allocating the proceeds to the underlying creditors fell upon our team.

Valuing IP assets in a bankruptcy setting is a common task asked of IP appraisers, but it is incredibly difficult to complete with any degree of accuracy. There are numerous factors when valuing IP assets, particularly patents. Explaining the depth of information and assumptions required to understand patent value is highly amorphous, so a book about the subject seemed the best way to educate regulators, administrators, judges, lawyers, investors, and entrepreneurs as to how it is done and how it can be made better.

When the America Invents Act (AIA) legislation became law in 2011, there were a lot of unknowns about the impact the AIA would have on the patent system. Most patent lawyers I knew were cautiously optimistic, but it was too early to know what would really happen.

In the twelve years since I conceived the idea of a book about IP and patents, the US patent system has undergone a remarkable transformation. The impact of that change has had a ripple effect on the broader startup community, which is a bigger part of the story than just patents or copyrights. For early-stage companies looking to become the next unicorn, the cautionary tales of startups that do not become unicorns are a warning to all founders dreaming of becoming the next Uber, DoorDash, or Stripe.

For every successful startup, nine failed startups never earn a meaningful return on investment. For the subsegment of start-ups that seek patent protection but do not have a meaningful exit, the patents they receive become a liability due to the legislative changes that occurred under the AIA. For that reason, most venture capital (VC) funds askew patents as unimportant and not necessary.

In the years since the AIA became law, the ramifications are now clear. Individuals, small companies, and universities have been on the wrong side of the law. The trials and tribulations that Inventors have lived through have been life-changing. I have witnessed firsthand the massive regulatory changes within the US IP system and have explored the corners of the IP system that many people are not aware of. Because of the problems I have witnessed, I write this book as a grave warning, with the hope that systematic change can reshape the US economy to achieve a more balanced, less adversarial relationship between the behemoth companies and the smaller upstarts.

Since IP is only partially defined and agreed upon, the average American has only a cursory understanding and knowledge of its existence, and most do not realize how impactful IP is on society. People make and use IP all the time, but it exists under the surface in thousands of unseen ways. Because of this, IP is often mistreated as a below-the-radar asset that is confusing and confounding to businesspeople. This confusion creates conflict that makes the valuation and pricing of IP assets extraordinarily difficult. Through the confusion, massive companies can develop technology platforms that provide outsized returns by using another IP owner's IP assets without permission. This book outlines these inherent problems and provides a suggestion for dramatically improving the system through digital modernization.

The rise of Big Tech has come at the great expense of the

United States patent system. Given my "in the trenches" work with patent holders of all sizes, I have a unique vantage point compared to most practitioners in finance. What I have witnessed has been so vile and untoward that I am compelled to write my stories, which will take me years to unpack.

This first book I have written deals exclusively with the problems of the US patent system. More specifically, I will tell the stories of two individual Inventors, Ray Yarris and Satoshi Noda (aliases), who have been wronged by infringers with deep pockets. Their stories of IP theft are not unique, and the aggregated count of the small and individual Inventors who have been dismayed by the US patent system has become endemic.

Said differently, individual Inventors have lost faith in the US patent system, and if they stop patenting, big companies will have no reason to continue to patent. If not corrected, the system could implode if not fixed. Thankfully, the combination of new leadership at the United States Patent and Trademark Office (USPTO) in deputy director, Coke Morgan Stewart, and newly appointed USPTO director, John Squires, has a different view than the prior administration. Stewart and Squires, along with the secretary of commerce, Howard Lutnick, are bringing meaningful reform to the patent system.

There is a better way, but it starts with recognizing the system's problems, which are finally being seen. This is the start of my explanation of how to fix the US patent system using existing techniques and methods widely accepted by the patent community, regulators, and the US accounting system.

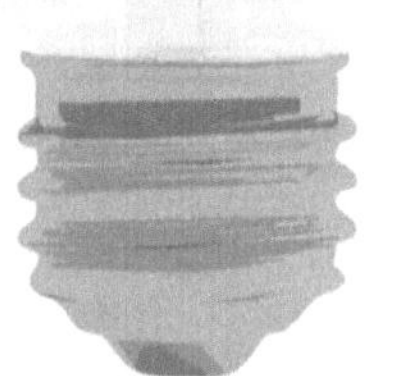

RAY YARRIS AND TECHNOLOGY, IP, AND PATENT VALUATION

HOW FINANCE EXPLAINS THE BROKEN US PATENT SYSTEM

"The amount of energy needed to refute bullshit is an order of magnitude bigger than that required to produce it."

—BRANDOLINI'S LAW (A.K.A. THE BULLSHIT ASYMMETRY PRINCIPLE)

MONEY MAKES THE WORLD GO ROUND

Black Monday, October 19, 1987, set the US stock market reeling. The Dow Jones lost 22 percent in the largest financial market decline since 1929, the catalyst of the Great Depression. It was a moment that stuck in my childhood mind and made me curious about finance. It was my first real and vivid memory of seeing the stock market indices and I was drawn to how an invisible force could produce such significant repercussions throughout society. The TV news showed the traders on the New York Stock Exchange floor, devastated, some of the traders crying. It seemed almost unfathomable to my ten-year-old mind.

Nearly forty years later, that day flashes in my mind like a cycling movie. Black Monday is a core memory in my psyche and the boom-and-bust economic cycles are part of the fabric of the US economy. With every new financial crisis, my memory hearkens back to Black Monday, a devasting yet figurative explosion that changed the trajectory of my life toward finance.

It was just a day, like any other day. A passing moment. A blip in the news. But Black Monday precipitated my father being laid off from his commercial banking job shortly after. Black Monday was the tipping of a domino that created a series of unfortunate events in my life. The experience of my childhood and bearing witness to the financial, emotional, and mental hardship my family went through during the loss of my father's job left a deep impression on me.

My father was a pious and frugal man who took the bus to work downtown from the suburbs, and he would walk home from the bus stop every day. Sometimes, I would greet him at the end of the street on his walk home. It was usually a joyous occasion where I would run as fast as I could, he would put down his briefcase, I would jump into his arms, and he would swing me around. However, on a random day shortly after Black Monday, he was walking home when I was with my friends, outside playing. I did not do my normal run-up for a hug. Instead, I just stopped and said hi.

"I will be home soon," I told him.

"Sounds good. Have fun and be safe," he responded.

In hindsight, it was too early in the day. The sun was still out, and I found out later that evening that he had been laid off. My mom was devastated, and my father was in shock. My sister retreated to her room, and I just sat there with my dad, with no idea what to do or say.

"Everything is going to be okay," he told me. But it was not.

It took my father a long time to find his next job. It wore on his psyche, especially as my mom's wholesale marketing business started taking off. She had landed an account with a big warehouse retailer and was making decent money for the first time. It emasculated my father, and by the time he found a new job seven months later, the marriage was a wreck.

I pinpoint Black Monday as being the precursor to the eventual demise of my parents' marriage. Black Monday led to the layoffs of thousands of people in the banking industry, including my dad. The strain of an already rocky marriage hit the skids after the layoff. I expect that if my father had not been fired, something else would have ended the marriage, but maybe not? It is one of those lingering questions I will never know the answer to.

All that aside, the infamous seed of "finance" was planted in my mind. Finance would become my calling, and the seed was planted on Black Monday in 1987. In college, I studied finance at Colorado State University. My first real job after graduating was working on an institutional trading floor for bonds at Robert W. Baird, an investment bank in Milwaukee, Wisconsin.

INSTITUTIONAL TRADING

Perched on the twenty-fourth floor of Milwaukee's tallest building, my desk looked northeast toward Lake Michigan. I sat on the trading desk for the institutional bond traders and provided research support to the sales team. Making a market to transact "fixed income" or bond securities was the core function of the trading desk, and when cheap bonds became available, the traders would look to my team to figure out if the bond issuer could make the interest payments, and pay back the debt when it came due. Cheap bonds are usually a signal of distress, and buying them below costs (or par value) meant the market thought they might default. For many institutional money managers, trading away potential risk was necessary to hitting targeted returns on investment (ROIs).

Fixed-income money managers, such as pension funds, insurance companies, hedge funds, or other large retirement services investment groups, rely upon institutional trading desks to help keep large investment portfolios aligned with the prospectuses provided to investors. Despite all the media attention paid to the equity markets, the institutional bond markets are multiple orders of magnitude larger than the equity markets. Equities make the news, but bonds and fixed income make corporate business and government go round.

Being on a trading desk at age twenty-two seemed like a dream come true. I had only read about what it would be like to be a "market maker" of an issued investment security, and now I was witnessing bond transactions in the millions of dollars every few hours.

In 1999, bond trading was still a ticket-printing business. Transactions were completed through a ticket printing process that was analog. Technology was too early to transact bonds solely electronically, and I was witnessing the last remnants of a dying transaction method. Actual tickets being printed for institutional bond traders ended at my firm by late 2000. The end of printed tickets, and the age of digital transactions, brought out a lot of nostalgia on the trading desk.

"Remember when everyone smoked at their desks?" one salesman remarked.

"Oh, those were the good days. We always kept a bottle of

scotch under the desk too," said the trader at the Bloomberg terminal next to him, his eight screens glowing.

"Damn it! What I wouldn't givvvve for a cigarette right now!" cried Jim Kohan, senior fixed income economist, as he slammed his fist on the desk.

Everyone busted out laughing hysterically. This is what it was like most of the time on the bond trading desk: laughs, gossip, and jokes. But for about 20 percent of the time, the traders and sales guys got their game faces on and transacted large block bond investments—millions to tens of millions of dollars in bonds traded at a time.

Bonds, a form of debt, typically carry less risk than equities. Bonds are also more thinly traded, making them more or less volatile, depending on the company's financial returns. Watching the equity markets is more entertaining than observing the bond market because the volumes whipsaw the market, but with bonds, there is a lot less action.

Bonds are expected to be paid back, and for most stable companies, issuing bonds is basically like taking a bank loan out but to several banks at one time. Investment banks help to organize and underwrite debt offerings, and I sat on a desk that helped facilitate the sale of both initial debt offering and secondary debt trading. As the investment bank underwriting the debt, we were market makers for secondary trading. Platforms for trading financial securities have changed dramatically over the years, but it was slow to be adopted at an institutional level.

When the salespeople's clients (i.e., large money managers) needed to buy or sell specific positions in their portfolios, the bond traders were there to facilitate the transactions. Facilitating a market for bonds was like being assigned to watching a glacier. Slow. Boring. Then a huge chunk breaks, and it causes a spur of activity to help a salesperson's client, and then back to relative calm.

I was a lowly financial analyst sitting next to Jim Kohan, a thirty-year Wall Street professional who had previously managed a bond fund with $20 billion in assets under management (AUM). He was a big deal until a trade went sideways on him.

"Give me a computer and a monkey, and I'll give you a financial analyst," he told me the first day I met him in the office. Jim was a Wisconsin native who moved to New York City in the 1970s to make his mark in the finance industry. He was a short man with thick-rimmed glasses and slicked-down, parted grey and blonde hair. His voice was raspy from years of smoking at his desk in the 1970s and '80s, something he gave up because they "forced" him to.

Jim was in the twilight of his career, and produced a publication called *Fixed Income Weekly* for the sales team's clients. Rumor had it he lost tens of millions of other people's money in a trade gone bad. The trade was so bad it closed down his investment fund. Of course, it was never confirmed to me, but he left New York and came home to Wisconsin a few years before I got there. He was not managing money anymore, except his own account. His daily activity consisted of coming in early, watching the markets, trading his own account, writing for a few hours, and leaving around 1:00 p.m. to go work out. We were strange bedfellows.

The Baird team had about fifty institutional bond (fixed income) traders and salesmen who created a market for investment funds looking to transact bond securities. The bond sales guys called on investment managers who oversaw billions invested in retirement funds or insurance companies, money that required capital preservation with passive income from interest payments or dividends.

Every month, insurance companies receive billions through the monthly premiums they collect for the insurance policies they underwrite. Those premiums are then invested into fixed-income securities that will earn a return but also can be easily converted (or liquidated) into cash if disastrous claims are made. The desk I sat on helped facilitate the market to transact the bond securities being held by insurance companies' investment portfolios.

When the traders moved in and out of bond positions sold to the salespeople's clients, the big block transactions produced commissions that doubled or tripled my entire year's salary. Selling a bond block of $10 million bonds was an occasional occurrence, resulting in a commission of $50,000 to $300,000. It was a remarkable thing to witness, and I was keen to join the trading team, but then the dot-com bubble burst in March 2000.

The second financial market crash in my lifetime led to the first financial crisis of my career. The dot-com bubble popped because of the "irrational exuberance" of the market in chasing dot-com company returns. Unlike the financial crises that would come in 2008 and again in 2020, the 2000 dot-com crash was a slow-moving financial trainwreck, littered with a variety of disasters like 9/11, Enron's failure, and the implosion of the Big 5 accounting firm, Arthur Andersen. The fallout from these horrible situations and financial disasters changed the permanent trajectory of my career from investment banking to business and intellectual property valuation.

"NECESSITY IS THE MOTHER OF INVENTION"

The second enlightenment I took away from my adolescence was an affinity for *Star Trek*, and science fiction. The idea of space travel and the ingenuity of building a space program fascinated me. Beyond the telling of celestial stories, the creative process of imagining the future with space exploration at the center made me a geek among my peers. What made me a nerd was my fascination with the inventions in the show that seemed almost implausible at the time. In high school, my obsession with *Star Trek: The Next Generation* led me to record every episode using my VCR. I would spend hours watching and rewatching episodes of shows, always fascinated with how the engineering department would solve the problems the crew encountered, usually by having a real-time talk with an artificial intelligence (AI)–enabled personal computer.

Gene Roddenberry and his team of writers were among the first to imagine the numerous devices we use today, including cell phones, tablets, touch screens, 3D printers, robotics, and AI. If imagined devices from *Star Trek* could be used as prior art in invention disclosures, many patented inventions may have never been issued. For many people involved in IP, *Star Trek* or other forms of science fiction became the original impetus for pursuing a career in engineering, technology, and IP.

Science and technology create complex ideas that can be transformed into a business operation that generates income. The patent system is the governing means by which the income generated from those inventions is allocated to the Inventor of those ideas, for a limited time. A patent is the means to incentivize all people within a society to create useful tools to promote economic progress for all people, but it comes with a trade—a "quid pro quo" where the trade-off of publicly disclosing an invention is that the government will provide a twenty-year exclusive right to use it. After twenty years, the patented technology becomes free to use by anyone (also known as expired or "off" patent). Patented technology has been a principle of commerce that has encouraged the greatest technological expansion in human history.

From that single thought, the idea of a bootstrapping American entrepreneur has been one of the most important and valuable economic engines over the last 250 years, but it has never been easy. Throughout American history, the strength of the United States Patent and Trademark Office (USPTO) swings like a long pendulum across decades and scores toward strength and weakness, depending on the changing legislative bodies. In this latest iteration of legislative change under the AIA, the US patent system is strained under its weakest position in the last half century, if not longer. Individual and small business Inventors have been ruthlessly and callously abused by a system that was initially enacted to prevent abuse, but has, in fact, elicited extraordinary abuse on individual and small business patent holders. What has occurred over the last fifteen years since the AIA became law has left the small Inventor class in stasis, shocked at the overwhelming abuse at the combined hands of the largest accused infringers, the USPTO, and the legislatures that continue to believe the debunked myth of patent trolls. The AIA has led many Inventors I know to hold intense feelings of dismay, anger, resentment, and, in some unfortunate cases, to suicide.

Invention is a fabled and noble task in the earliest picture of humanity's rise from early scavengers to its current bustling society. Humans love a good origin story, and invention almost always provides a great one.

The spark that makes the fire.

The chisel that makes the wheel.

The combustion engine that makes the locomotive.

The wings and engine that make the airplane.

The semiconductor chips that make the computer.

The operating system that makes the PC.

The network that connects the PCs.

Invention is an act of evolution that leads to revolutions, and humanity is experiencing technological waves at a faster pace than ever in human history. Theoretically, the IP protections afforded by society to everyone and anyone provide an incentive to build a better, more efficient society. The idea that every person in a country can contribute to the research and development (R&D) of the country's innovation is the qualifying force that enables equality and diversity. The writers of the US Constitution understood the importance of creative incentives, which is why the "promotion of useful science" is part of America's founding documents. The patent system was envisioned as part of the fabric of American life.

However, my experience with patented IP has shown that policies favoring large, multinational enterprises (MNEs) have undermined patent value, and reallocated technology value toward non-patented technology, like trade secrets and know-how. The returns earned on IP by large companies are often extraordinary, while patents have been systematically devalued. The dichotomy has hurt individuals, small company Inventors, and entrepreneurs who are often left to compete with deep-pocketed incumbents who create competing products at lower price points than smaller competitors. When the smaller competitors cry "foul" and attempt to enforce their patented rights, the "alleged" infringer will use the AIA's draconian invalidation process to remove the small company's patent from ever existing in the first place. Meanwhile, the alleged infringer is giving the technology away for free using income from a non-related business. Given societies' desire for "free" trials, large incumbents can effectively "buy" a market by drastically reducing a product's costs well below smaller competitors' break-even points.

A perfect example of this is the audio speaker market. Sonos, the portable speaker maker founded in 2004, pioneered wireless audio and home stereo systems, enabling wireless speakers to become ubiquitous nationwide. Sonos's original focus was on creating wireless speaker systems for home and travel that would enable seamless listening across devices. The digital revolution of music created unique opportunities to disrupt the speaker market, and Sonos was a first-mover in the space.

In 2016, twenty years after Sonos's launch, Google (and Amazon) entered the home speaker market. The Google Home speaker entered the market at a price point of $129, compared to the Sonos Play speaker, which sold for $199. Google's ability to price a similar product to Sonos created a highly competitive market for speakers. The lower-priced Google speaker created a pricing war that Sonos was unable to sustain. Google's size, reach, and network enables the ability to subsidize speaker pricing to capture market share. This example highlights early-stage companies' difficulty competing with massive companies like Google. Moreover, Google's ability to subsidize a lower-priced competing product is enabled by the tax savings incurred through transfer pricing. Sadly, the CEO of Sonos's fight against Google has not gone well, and Sonos stock price has suffered. In the summer of 2025, the CEO of Sonos resigned his role and the company is "hitting a hard reset" per *The Wall Street Journal*.

The more global the MNE, the more likely they are to use internally generated IP to reduce its effective tax rate using an esoteric technique called "transfer pricing." These advantages come at the indirect expense of smaller, innovative companies and individual Inventors. For small businesses trying to compete with large, deep-pocketed companies, the complexity, uncertainty, and (alleged) vast infringement creates a doomed universe of failed startups, many of which have their IP pilfered and used without authorization, like what happened to Sonos.

To put the final nail in the coffin for small Inventors, the AIA's Patent Trial and Appeal Board (PTAB, pronounced p-tab) has become known as the "patent death squad," where the inter partes review (IPR) process acts as an administrative tribunal to reconsider the validity of patent claims after they are granted. The IPR process allows anyone called a "petitioner" to challenge the claims of a patent's authenticity at any time after the patent has been granted. The ability to rechallenge a patent's claims after it was granted has always been a part of the patent process, but the AIA's IPR broadened the scope of the review process. While the IPR was promoted as a faster alternative to court litigation, the use of quasi-hindsight has proven challenging, and the invalidation rates have been in the high double digits since the IPR's inception in 2013. That is, until the interim director, Coke Morgan Stewart, started denying petitioners' IPRs through her discretionary denial powers, which Congress gave to the USPTO but which have been underutilized since IPR's launch in 2013.

The PTAB's IPR has been used to invalidate an extraordinary number of patents presented before the panel. These IPR proceedings often run in parallel with district court patent litigation proceedings and unequivocally add time and expense to the plaintiffs' case in a patent lawsuit.

All these issues have made climbing the hill of patented invention and innovation nearly impossible for the individual or small company. The unintended consequence of the AIA is an overtly lopsided playing field, catering to the richest, fastest-growing companies in the world, slowly killing the inventing community in the process.

The juxtaposition of a diminished patent system, while Big Tech companies reach all-time valuation highs, is one of the most underrepresented issues of our lifetime. Historically, individual Inventors in their garages, who have left the burdensome bureaucracies of large companies, have pushed American society faster and farther than at any point in history, but the incentives to take the same leap for new or undiscovered Inventors are declining.

Why?

Inventors, often, are introverts. In my twenty-five-year career, I have met Inventors from across the globe. I have listened to their stories of invention and creation to solve a specific problem for which they are subject matter experts. Inventors are analytical and logical, like Spock, the half-Vulcan and half-human from *Star Trek*. Science, technology, engineering, and math (STEM) are the backbone personalities of the inventing class, and their focus is extraordinarily astute compared to the rest of society. Driven focus on high-level problems often limits an Inventor's peripheral vision toward regulatory change, so Inventors had almost no idea how big the AIA change was until years after it had become law.

Inventors are driven to improve a process, task, or idea. Focused Inventors are usually poor businesspeople. The qualities that enable them to resolve issues creatively make them inversely skilled at becoming entrepreneurs. The iconic stories of Inventors like Steve Jobs, Elon Musk, Bill Gates, or Jeff Bezos are very rare. More likely, an Inventor is a brainiac with an understated personality. Moreover, many of the Inventors I have met admit to being on the autism spectrum, and they freely admit that business building is not even remotely plausible for them. And so, they invent, patent, and then it becomes a bloody nightmare to monetize, particularly when infringement is found.

Changes in legislative policy don't stop the eureka moments that have come to define invention. Inventors are everyone, and only through their natural curiosity does the discovery in their minds set on the light bulb. Literally, anyone can invent. In fact, most people create and implement their own inventions multiple times throughout their lives, but those are personal moments. It takes a unique kind of person to move from invention to the legal protection of the invention with a patent.

Only the government can grant a patent. Anyone can invent, but only the government issues the certificate that states an Inventor has an exclusive right to use an invention for the standard term, twenty years in the US. At the USPTO, nearly six hundred thousand applications are processed every year. Of those, around 30 percent to 45 percent become patents. It is an incredible dismissal grant rate, and many believe the current patent issuance rate is still too high.

Of the nearly 3.5 million currently active US patents granted as of 2026, an unknown number of those patents are being used in commercialized products. However, only a small portion of patents are being licensed or sold as standalone assets, and an even smaller number of those agreements are made public. That leaves individual and small company patent owners with the difficult challenge of protecting against unauthorized use of their patent rights through litigation. The AIA made patent litigation much harder, and the unintended consequences of the AIA have had a staggering cost to Inventors and the overall patent system itself.

As an IP and patent portfolio appraiser, I have witnessed firsthand the vast destruction the AIA has had on patent holders. Before the AIA became law, the US patent system was relatively strong. Patents granted were assumed to be valid, and the process for determining infringement had been relatively straightforward for decades. The process of "re-examination" that would remove the validity stamp from the USPTO was infrequently used, and hard to justify. Accordingly, patent litigation spiked from the early 2000s until 2011, when the AIA became law.

Once the AIA became law, the use of the PTAB cast a pall over the entire system. The AIA pushed the patent system into a recession, which transformed into a depression, and it is now in a phase of implosion.

For the anti-patent community, the demise of the patent system is welcome news. Inside the US, anti-patent advocates rely on the advice and counsel of academics to support their anti-patent stances toward invention. One semi-famous academic, Alex Tabarrok from George Mason University, has spent a portion of his career explaining how patents hinder innovation. Of course, Professor Tabarrok's anti-patent research viewpoints of invention and innovation are steeped in large company examples, primarily focusing on the impact of patents on institutional innovation. Absent from the research and understanding is the impact of a weakening patent system on early-stage companies, founders, and angel investors. Lost in the anti-patent academic research is the impact on individual and small company Inventors.

After years of abuse, many of the individual and small Inventors I know have given up on the US patent system. Seeking US patent protection does not work, and it is giving large incumbents a free ride. Unless the system is strengthened, the need for patents will ebb so low that the garage or basement Inventor will entirely give up hope in the system.

WHAT HOPE IS THERE FOR PATENT HOLDERS?

"Get a good attorney."

That was the advice of then–USPTO Director Andrei Iancu

when I asked him, "What do you say to inventors who were issued patents between 2000 and 2013 and believe their patents are infringed?"

Former Director Iancu might not remember our conversation at the LOT (License On Transfer) Network conference held in the opulent Palace Hotel in San Francisco in 2018, but his words have resonated with me ever since. He was not wrong, either. The US patent system is convoluted and complex, and it has gotten increasingly worse since the AIA became law.

CHAPTER 2

THE IP PYRAMID FORTRESS

"He who receives an idea from me, receives instruction himself without lessening mine; as he who lights his taper at mine, receives light without darkening me."

—THOMAS JEFFERSON

THE UNINTENDED CONSEQUENCES OF THE AIA, THE STORY OF RAY YARRIS

I first met Ray Yarris in 2013, about two years after his first patent had been issued. Ray applied for the patent in 2006, it had a priority date of 2007, and it was issued in 2011. It was a crowning achievement of his career to that point, or at least he thought it would be. Eventually, his patent would prove to be a curse that Ray could not quit.

Ray was born in 1970, the third of three boys. He had an immediate affinity for technology and tinkering. At age six, his parents bought him an Altair 8800, one of the first "build it yourself" personal computers ever offered. After turning it on, he discovered that it required DOS programming knowledge, and that is where Ray spent a lot of his free time: programming computers. When most eight-year-olds were outside playing baseball, Ray was inside learning DOS and building his operating systems.

By age fourteen, Ray had his first-ever paid computer programming job. A wiz with computers, Ray entered the engineering school at Indiana University in 1988, and before he could graduate, he was being offered lucrative computer programming opportunities from a variety of consulting firms.

By the late '90s, Ray became a database system architect for the National Security Agency (NSA), building massive database registries of foreign agents and the various entities associated with those agents. Most of the database was maintained by low-level programmers except for the trickier, thornier issues related to data transfer and storage capacity. In addressing the NSA's problems, Ray developed a new method for data transfer that significantly reduced the time and effort required for network capacity. Once his contract with the NSA ended in 2001, Ray was able to pursue a full working design for his data storage system freely.

Around the same time that Ray left the NSA, he met a woman and fell in love. By 2006, they had been married for five years and had three kids. Ray got along well with his wife's family, and his father-in-law (FIL) recognized Ray's exceptional skills as a programmer and encouraged him to use his skills to become an entrepreneur. Ray's FIL even financed his patent application and eventually helped launch his startup, Self-Server, in 2007.

This is where the timing of being too early caused Ray's startup to fail. The IP Ray created should have helped him, but the protections afforded to patent holders at that time became so weak after the AIA became law that the patents undermined his entire company.

THE INTELLECTUAL PROPERTY PYRAMID FORTRESS

IP is one of the cornerstones of free enterprise. The US patent and IP system is part of America's infrastructure, and it has been neglected at a fundamental level for generations. The legalized incentive to create ideas into commercialized enterprises is foundational to all countries, particularly democracies. Governments worldwide legislate IP protection to create incentives and business across four legally protected IP forms. The ripple impact that follows is how nations write their treaties around these forms of IP protection.

Analogies and metaphors about IP vary widely, but having spent my entire career thinking about the value and price of IP, I have a unique viewpoint. IP is a "Pyramid Fortress" of protection related to ideas, inventions, and concepts. The government grants IP, and the IP Pyramid Fortress is a metaphorical fortress that is the policy governments enact to protect IP. Under most government regimes, legally protected IP will undergo varied phases of relative strength or weakness. The pendulum swings from strength to weakness slowly, taking decades or longer. From the early 1980s through 2010, America's IP protections were considered the gold standard for modeling an IP system and had experienced significant strength during that time.

That strength flipped after the AIA was enacted, and the patent system has weakened considerably since 2013. For Inventors, their protection under the patent wall has eroded, and technology creation has shifted to other forms of IP protection. Since IP is most valuable when the four walls of IP operate collectively with company synergies, the fortress's walls come to a point at the top, making the pyramid. The four walls of the IP Pyramid Fortress include the following for almost all countries that have IP laws:

1. Patents
2. Trade secrets
3. Copyrights
4. Trademarks / Trade names

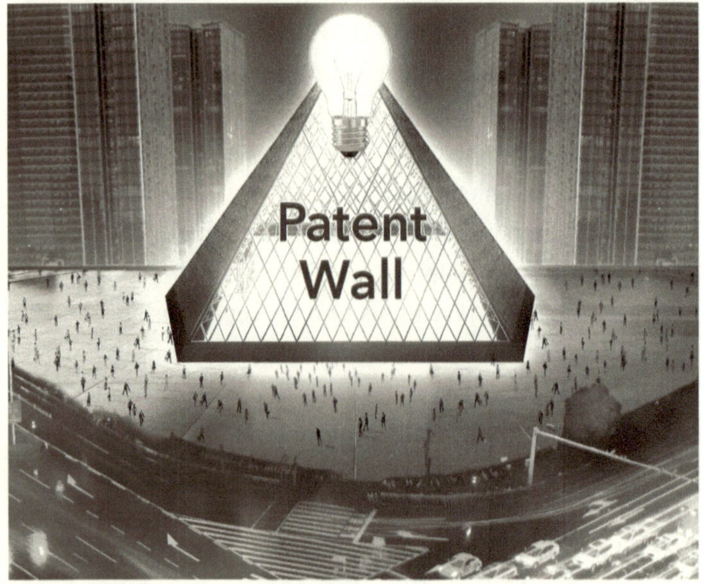

Figure 1: Illustrative rendering of IP Pyramid Fortress

Each of the four walls comprises the government policy for legally protecting IP classes. The intent for all four IP walls is largely the same: *to incentivize the creation of arts, sciences, and the pursuit of innovation.* Provide any ordinary citizen the right to create an idea into a popularly adopted thing, whether it is music, a story, a brand, or an invention, and compensation for the commercialization of IP will financially lift the most creative members of its population. And for the most part, it has worked exceptionally well for three out of the four walls. Patents, however, have fluctuated through periods of relative strength and weakness, which have disproportionately impacted Inventors compared to other IP creators.

Numerous industries have flourished under the protection of the IP Pyramid Fortress. IP protection has helped forge industries and incentivize business creation for centuries. Legal IP assets have worked to varying degrees of usefulness in spurring economic activity. According to the USPTO, 127 IP-intensive industries in sectors such as manufacturing, wholesale and retail trade, professional, technical, management, and administrative services accounted for $7.8 trillion in US gross domestic product (GDP), or 41 percent of total GDP.

Typically, IP protection from industry participants strengthens and improves legal IP protections, but patents are a different story. The US patent system's strength can cause problems for large incumbent enterprises, most notably through the rise of "patent trolls" in the early 2000s. "Patent troll" is the pejorative name for "non-practicing entities" or NPE and can be interchanged with "patent assertion entities" or PAEs. Due to the significant increase in patent litigation from the mid-1990s through 2011, criticizing patent owners who are not Implementers of commercialized products has become commonplace.

Most of the well-known NPEs, such as Intellectual Ventures, WiLAN, Conversant, Acacia, Marathon Patent Group, and several others, have all transitioned away from patent monetization as their primary means of business. To that degree, the impact of the AIA has gone exactly as planned. However, in its place are rogue operators with skeleton crews that mass enforce a handful of powerful patent families, like patent bounty hunters. PAEs in the 2020s include entities like IP Edge or Fortress Investment Group, which operate as patent buyers of last resort for hundreds of sellers who believe their patents carry intrinsic value through litigation. NPEs or PAEs see tens of thousands of patent monetization opportunities every year, but only a very small portion of those reviewed assets can become qualified patents for enforcement and monetization.

Unenforceable patents have become the norm in patent monetization efforts. While damages outcomes have improved for patent holders the last few years, outsized damages from patent litigations seen in the 2000s and early 2010s are no longer likely. In fact, if a patent holder manages to win in litigation, the likelihood of being paid remains low because the infringer can delay payment through the Federal Circuit appeal process. Winning patent infringement cases makes actual damages payments to patent holders a multiyear-long task to collect. Even worse, the Federal Circuit has been known to overturn jury verdicts and/or slash the payment decisions from lower courts that would have been a benefit to patent owners.

The AIA ushered in a new wave of patent weakness. The ebbs and flows of IP strength and weakness over the last fifty years in the US are highlighted by a chart from the Center for IP Understanding, which follows.

The Footprints of Patent History

Understanding the history of key patent events, and the ups and downs of patent reliability over the past 50 years, helps to put their current difficulties into perspective.

1970s
Relatively Low Use

- Rise of Japanese electronics, autos
- Restrictive antitrust rules limit licensing
- Microsoft, Apple established

1980s
Higher Certainty

- Bayh-Dole (1980)
- CAFC established (1982)
- Univ tech transfer grows
- IBM enters PC market
- *Polaroid v. Kodak* ($1B)
- Chakrabarty (life sciences)

1990s
High Certainty

- Licensing activity grows
- Higher damages awarded for infringement
- ED and WDTX emerge
- Google founded (pat. # 6,678,681)
- Rise of China counterfeits

2000s
Highest Certainty

- *eBay* case (2006)
- Smartphone wars begin
- "Troll" meme spreads
- Licensing peaks
- China IP theft grows
- AST, RPX, LOT Network established

2010s
Lowering Certainty

- AIA enacted (2011)
- PTAB established (2012)
- SCOTUS narrows eligible patents
- "Efficient" infringement grows

- Patent reliability down
- Tech licensing down
- Litigation flat
- Indie inventors struggle
- China surpasses US filings by 18% in 2023

Figure 2: The Footprint of Patent History

In 2011, the patent system in America underwent a significant shift toward general patent weakness with the enactment of the AIA, and US patents have not been the same since. The slow degradation of patent strength has been part of the country's general shift toward keeping consumer costs low and benefits high. Large companies that have less onerous IP restrictions can more easily monetize their customer base. In an era of building large user bases that become customers, "giveaways" and free access to a product or service require weaker IP rights and low-cost entry points to build users. Large companies with a strong user base can tap into their customer network and determine the winners and losers of technology at much lower costs, particularly if they can use someone else's patented technology for free.

Once a critical mass of users is created, monetization becomes nearly like turning on a faucet. Active users receiving goods or services on a platform create "viral" moments, where users are activated into buying. Amazon has perfected this with its annual Prime Day, an annual summer sale that provides exceptional "savings" across the e-commerce site. The activation of Prime Day results in some of Amazon's largest volume days besides the Christmas season.

The ability to amass global events through the sale of products has created iconic billionaires, many of whom are named, patented Inventors. Meanwhile, there's been a slow-motion dismantling of patent rights that has eroded the patent strength of thousands of individual and small company Inventors. The patent system's debasement to the detriment of individual Inventors and small companies for the benefit of big business is brazenly apparent, but since it has changed slowly over time, it seems barely noticeable.

NON-PATENTED, LEGAL IP ASSETS

The second wall of the IP Pyramid Fortress is trade secrets. Conversely, to patents, trade secret protection was boosted during the Obama administration after the Defend Trade Secrets Act (DTSA) of 2016. Enforcement activities in the court system have risen since the DTSA became law, and numerous experts have pointed to corporate efforts to strengthen trade secret practices. Many IP experts believe this offsets the weakening of patents and that if companies focus on trade secrets, weakened patents will matter less to enterprises. I think this is foolhardy and wishful thinking.

In reality, trade secrets are not the inverse of a patent. Patents stand on their own because invention is often a race, and the process of patenting an invention was designed to be the first to invent. Trade secrets, on the other hand, are supposed to be difficult to replicate. If an Inventor decides not to patent his invention, but rather keep it as a trade secret, he runs the risk of a competitor reverse engineering his trade secrets and taking the IP for its own, allowing for the secret to be squandered. Therefore, a patent is disclosed to limit the competitor from taking the invention through his own skilled abilities. Even the strongest of trade secret protection is not immune to reverse engineering. The truth is, a weakened patent system weakens trade secret protections as well.

The third wall, copyrights, has been controversial for some time. Copyright laws in the US are meaningfully stronger than patent laws. Violate copyrights against Hollywood, Disney, or *The New York Times*, and criminal prosecution is not out of the question. When you agree to stream movies on your device, you consent to not copying the media's copyright for financial gain, and copying carries criminal prosecution. However, no one has ever been threatened with prison for stealing patented technology, at least not in the US.

Most recently, AI companies have used copyrighted material to train their systems. This has resulted in numerous copyright lawsuits against OpenAI, Anthropic, Perplexity AI, Google's Gemini, and many others. However, musical artists, Hollywood writers and actors, and college sports athletes seeking NIL (name, image, likeness) rights are all protected under copyright law (or sometimes trademark law), and the regulatory agencies are providing this protection. Copyright protection will continue to be a contentious IP asset, but the degradation of copyright laws in the US will meet a much stiffer counter-lobbying effort than the patent system did from 2005 to 2011.

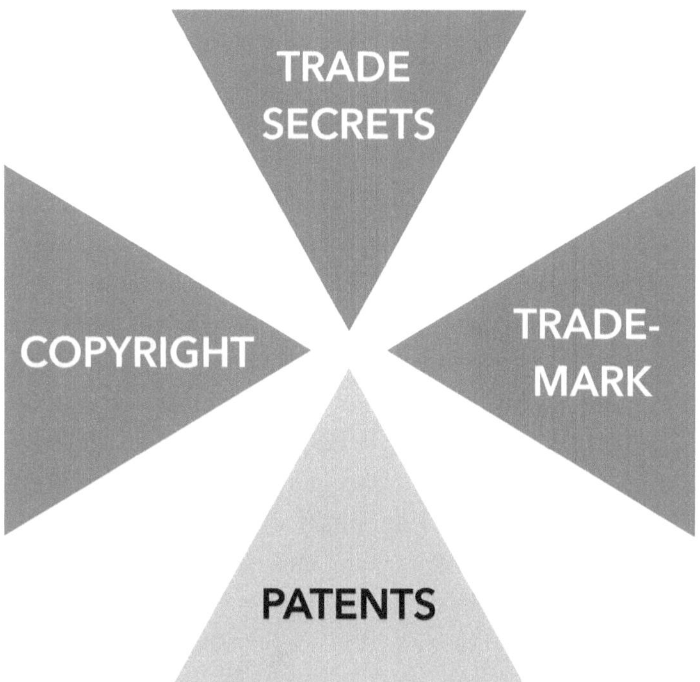

Figure 3: Bird's eye-view of the metaphorical IP Pyramid Fortress

The fourth wall of the IP Pyramid Fortress is trademark protection. Brands are the easiest IP protection to understand, and trademarks are the backbone of any brand. Branding helps promote business, and enforcement of trademark misuse is clearest to recognize and prevent. While controversies arise, the protection system and adjudication of unauthorized use of trademark and brands are reasonably straightforward. Controversies exist, but they are generally resolvable.

That returns us to the first wall of IP protection: patents. What has happened to patents since the AIA became law is a different issue. The passing of the AIA unleashed a series of unintended consequences that have brutalized Inventors through relentless attacks by classifying patent enforcement as "patent trolling." With no nuance or consideration, the Inventor community has undergone a brutal attack that has been generally underreported, trivialized, and dismissed. The AIA has given patent infringers cover to take patented technology with minimal consequences while undermining the value of patents for all participants in the US patent system.

As a financier, I immediately recognized patent trolling as a form of financial arbitrage. Not the most ethical means of profit-taking, but a financial edge not used leaves money on the table. So, patent trolls became a cottage industry that grew into a national outrage. By 2010, there was bipartisan support for patent reform. The lobbyist helping to write the legislation did not understand the impact of all the changes they were making, but they pushed it through anyway. Still, with over $1 billion of lobbying dollars going into the passage of the AIA, the Big Tech industry policy lobbyists put in everything they possibly could to undermine the US patent system.

I do not recall the day the AIA passed, but I remember when it went into effect: September 2011. Most industry participants wanted to hail it as a significant step forward for patent holders! The biggest feature (bug) of the system has been the PTAB, which would become known as the "patent death squad," resulting in small business and individual patent Inventors screaming *foul* at the top of their lungs once the PTAB was enacted.

In the fifteen years since the AIA became law, the patent wall in the IP Pyramid Fortress has weakened considerably. Brick-by-brick, decision-by-decision, and whitepaper-after-whitepaper unite to undermine granted patents across all sectors. The AIA's PTAB process became the means to allow anyone the chance to invalidate another person's patent. Granted patents are valid in name only. Once a patent holder attempts to enforce its rights, the patent owner must expect its patent's validity to be reconsidered through the PTAB.

"Efficient infringement" is a term used to describe how Implementers strategically utilize third-party patented technology without paying royalty fees. While patents are supposed to be a right to exclude, the US Supreme Court's ruling in *eBay Inc. v. MercExchange, L.L.C.* limited injunctions to occur only in limited circumstances after applying a four-factor test. These four factors have effectively ended injunctions for patent holders, giving Implementers and alleged infringers another means to free ride on other people's inventions. With the threat of an injunction greatly diminished, alleged infringers then receive the advantage of petitioning the PTAB to invalidate a patent's claims.

The attempt to invalidate a granted patent is made through the institution of an inter partes review (IPR), which subjects the patent to a new validation process that has a different interpretation premise than during the original prosecution of the patent. During a patent's initial prosecution, the USPTO patent examiner reviews the claims of a patent using a "broadest reasonable interpretation" (BRI) standard of review. The BRI standard used by patent examiners reviews the requirements for patentability, including novelty, nonobviousness, and utility. This allows for the broadest scope of patent claims, but it is necessary for the examiner to help clarify and narrow the claims prior to its granting.

In the IPR process, however, the three-judge panel reviewers use an interpretation of patent claims under a "preponderance of the evidence" standard. Under the preponderance of the evidence standard, a "more likely than not" outcome will tip the findings in favor of alleged infringers. The stricter standard in IPR proceedings has resulted in an exceptionally high number of "instituted" patents becoming invalid after the petition for IPR has been accepted.

If the PTAB decides the patent is invalid, the loss of the patent is complete and absolute. Since the PTAB became law, thousands of once-granted patents have been invalidated. In fact, the rate of invalidation is stunningly high (70 percent to 85 percent per year), begging the question of whether any of the patents being issued by the USPTO are valid in the first place. With the dual standards of evidence being applied at different times in a patent's life, is it any wonder why so many patents are invalidated?

Sadly, the IPR invalidation process almost always occurs when the patent holder needs their enforcement rights the most: when there is infringement and unauthorized use. Rather than put the patent's claims at the center of a dispute, the PTAB's process vacates the patent, and the invalidation makes it so that the patent never existed in the first place. The patent vanishes, and all the time, effort, expense, business plans, and expectations go "poof" upon an invalidation outcome. It is a killer of certainty in a patent asset. It is a systematic flaw purposefully injected into the patent process whose primary benefit is to enable serial infringement by incumbents. And it makes valuing and pricing patent portfolios a fool's errand.

Unfair and unjust describes how devastating the PTAB process is to patent owners. Watching its draconian impact on the Inventor community over the last fourteen years has been traumatizing. For patent holders granted patents from 2000 until 2010, the idea of PTAB was unfathomable. So, when the PTAB process went into law in 2013, professionals in the space waited with bated breath about the law's impact on businesses and Inventors. Fourteen years later, we know. Devastation.

At least for individuals and small company Inventors, the AIA has been devastating. For large operating companies, it has been a boon for operations. The slow dismantling of patent trolls has alleviated significant pressure on large corporations that have been happy to use the IPR process to stop patent licensing requests. Despite the significant retrenchment of patent trolls, the anti-patent activists continue to paint patent litigation as a boogeyman sent to destroy operating companies.

Many of the old guard patent trolls from the 2010s have had their roles shifted and changed. IP attorneys who formerly worked for patent trolls are often later hired by Big Tech companies. The revolving door of professionals operating in the patent space offers equal opportunity across the chasm of patent holder versus Implementer. For one job, an in-house IP attorney may be excoriating patents as being destructive to operating business. In the next job, the same IP attorney will assert patents against an operating company, extolling the virtues of the patent system. For many IP attorneys I know, their personal practice operates like a chameleon, changing their tunes depending on which side of the dispute they work.

To a certain degree, patent trolls have morphed into patent litigation funding groups. Once a nascent business, litigation funding has become a multibillion-dollar industry. Of all the types of litigation funding cases available, patent litigation makes up the largest number of offerings to these types of funders. However, because the US patent system has weakened so intolerably, it is the least funded type of opportunity. This leaves limited options for individuals and small businesses to monetize their patents if they cannot navigate traditional commercialization methods. It has caused many Inventors to question the value of their patent assets. If patents cannot be funded to enact patent litigation when infringement is present, the need for a patent is called into question.

If individuals and small businesses stop patenting, the process will eventually slow to a halt, and most innovation will only come from the most prominent companies, which is not ideal. Most American genius Inventors and entrepreneurs come from modest backgrounds, and limited means. Under the current convoluted patent system, individual Inventors and entrepreneurs are losing out. The loss of individual and small company Inventors will slow innovation by limiting the total number of Inventors willing to be included in the process. The patent system is meant to make the world an R&D center, but under its current form, it is disincentivizing Inventors to patent in the US.

To re-incentivize the world's Inventors, the patent wall in the IP Pyramid Fortress needs to be rebuilt and reconceptualized. The system has failed and created a patent system that favors only the largest, deepest-pocketed companies, where serial infringement occurs regularly, is widely accepted, and is fiercely defended. To address these actions, a new paradigm for patents is needed that will transform how IP is transacted, licensed, and accounted for. Regulation and auditing of IP utilized in commercialized products can strengthen the patent system into a fair playing field for all stakeholders. At the center of the system will be income directly tied to the patented technology granted by the government.

While the definition of a patent is the right to exclude others from using it, the opposite side of the coin is the right to license the patent technology. Licensing rights and the income they produce are the base core foundation of IP and patent valuation. By creating a system that more accurately associates IP rights with income, IP rights can become a financial derivative that operates and exists as a financial security. In fact, the financialization of IP rights could revolutionize capital allocation by incentivizing the best technology to be used in products, rather than the work-around that is the second- or third-best technical method.

Throughout my years of valuing and appraising businesses and IP, the most important value factor is cash flow. While there are other contributing factors to IP value, cash flow from IP is the most salient and crucial financial figure when estimating patent value. Proving cash flow from IP assets is challenging, but it is the basis for all patent litigation damages and awards calculations. Absent a direct tie to cash flow, IP value is highly subjective and changes depending on the situation. If cash flow is explicitly attributed to IP, such as a royalty fee, then the value of the IP can easily be calculated.

After the cash flow has been established, a transactional market for patent assets is feasible. Absent the direct tie of cash flow, a transactional market is a black box, and the valuation and pricing of patent assets are dislocated. Accordingly, the value of patents is amorphous and case-specific. It creates a marketplace where information asymmetry becomes the negotiating tactic used to delay, and the process of patent monetization is slowed to a near-grinding halt.

In an era when commodity assets have been monetized through platform marketplaces for trading, IP has moved backward and away from such progress. Assets like event tickets, carbon emissions, gift cards, accounts receivable, and cryptocurrency are all examples of assets that have a liquid, transactable market via the internet. Those commodity assets were challenging to transact on a secondary market a decade ago. Since then, a secondary transaction market has been created, resulting in more robust liquidity and transaction ability, but not so for patents and IP. The market for transacting patent assets is shrinking relative to the size of the entire patent market, and the USPTO has been there to covertly hamper a patent transaction market all along the way.

Why has it become this way? The short answer is regulatory capture. A collective group of companies, Big Tech, has the same problem—patent trolls—and they have pushed a regulatory transformation of the USPTO to favor Big Tech under the false guise of protecting startups. It is as simple as that.

HARD, SOFT, AND GREY IP ASSETS

Legally protected IP can be considered "hard" IP assets, meaning there is defined legal protection and the government has agencies set up for the specific purposes of issuing hard IP. Soft IP assets, on the other hand, are harder to define. The list of soft IP assets ranges from distribution networks to customer contracts to employee know-how. Soft IP assets are generally not tradable unless they are part of a larger enterprise, or unless bundled with a collection of assets. For example, IBM may decide that a group of software engineers in a specific division is no longer needed, and the engineering group could be fired or potentially sold to a competitor. The engineers, their knowledge, and their ability to execute have wildly different values depending on whether the group is given a severance or expected to continue operations with the company that acquired them. That fungible decision creates the "soft" aspect of the IP within that group.

Hard IP assets can be enforced with a much stronger stick. Use a trademark without authorization, and expect an IP lawyer to shut down the unauthorized use. Organizations with meaningful brands or copyrights, such as Coke, Netflix, Universal, or Disney, have large swathes of IP attorneys scouring the world for unauthorized use.

Grey IP sits in the middle and includes assets like software, contracts, schematic designs, engineering plans, databases, or other IP assets that could be transferred to a third party through sale or license but are difficult to enforce potential infringement through legal means. Reverse engineering grey IP assets is expensive or impossible. Hard IP assets are useful in protecting grey IP assets, and often, the combination of the two creates the most valuable IP in the world.

When done right, legally protected IP provided by the IP Pyramid Fortress allows the grey and soft IP assets to reach their highest and best value, like crown jewels. When deconstructing the value of IP, the richest threads are almost always the grey IP assets, which provide the most direct means of commercializing products and services, and it accounts for the largest portion of profit margin. The soft IP assets support an enterprise, and the hard IP assets act as a shield of protection against copying. But it is the profit margin that is afforded to an IP owner that fundamentally creates the most value for its owner.

At least, that is how it should be.

Intellectual Property Assets by Strength and Type

IP Type	Monetizable through trade or license?	Developed Technology	Marketing	Content	Information and Developed Technology
Hard IP	Easiest but still hard	Patents	Trademarks	Copyright	Trade secrets
Gray IP	Hard to challenge	Contracts, SDK, APIs	Brands, designs, promotions	Software source code, technical libraries, data collections	Schematics, design plans, recipes, corporate strategy
Soft IP	Difficult to impossible	Know-how, people, execution	Concepts, websites, social media, influencers	Written or verbal words supporting the business in any way	Know-how, people, execution, relationships

Figure 4

Developed Technology is a loosely defined accounting term under US GAAP (generally accepted accounting procedures). By "loosely," I mean that the company will define its Developed Technology value as it sees fit. And each accounting firm has its own definition of Developed Technology, which includes patented and unpatented technology. Or, as the box shows, "Developed Technology" may include the examples in the categories of IP in Figure 4.

In reality, patented technology represents only a small portion of the overall value of a product or service. Many factors influence technology, and patents are only one aspect of the broader value that enables a product or service. If an Implementer became a willing licensee that apportioned patented technology in good faith, third-party patented technology may become an even smaller fraction of the revenue of a product based on market participant negotiations. However, the backlash against patents and the system that dictates declaring all asserted patents as patent trolling has ushered in an era of invalidation rather than compensation for use.

Since the AIA, the patent system has been degrading its most vulnerable group: the individual and small company Inventors. It has limited the advancement of early-stage companies for the benefit of the largest companies. The unintended consequences of the AIA have been stark and disconcerting.

While the American Inventor has always faced an uphill battle to move through the phases of invention, it has become harder than ever due to the AIA. From the initial stages of invention to proof of concept and eventually to commercialized success, it is a tricky endeavor in the best of circumstances. Technology changes with incredible quickness, and simultaneous invention occurs regularly across several industries.

This is the nature of evolutionary technological progress. The human capacity for understanding and invention is stimulated through measured, competitive progress. Because of the pace of discovery, dueling inventions by different people at different locations occur regularly, and the patent office sorts through those applications, issuing patents to the first to file for a patent rather than the first to invent, as had been the case in the US, pre-AIA. Given the broad changes to the US patent system since the AIA, trying to fully understand the impact of these changes can be confusing. Understanding these changes and their economic impact on society at large is critical to adjusting the system so that it is a fair and level playing field for all involved.

CHAPTER 3

THE PATENT WARS NEVER ENDED

"You don't need a formal conspiracy when interest converges."

—GEORGE CARLIN, COMEDIAN

THE CLOUD: BUILDING A NEW INDUSTRY

In 2005, the idea of "the cloud" was not yet widely accepted. Amazon's S3 services were only a minuscule portion of their overall business. Still, it was clear that renting out server space for enterprises (also known as the cloud) would be a major opportunity in the future. For all of Ray Yarris's genius with computer programming, his understanding of how an enterprise would address server capacity was off the mark. This happens with engineers and Inventors: They're keen to create and invent but not always astute with running a business. Ray's calculated mistake was that consumers and in-house information technology (IT) staff would build out larger network storage racks on-site rather than rely on the cloud.

In early 2008, Ray founded Self-Server, a software service for storing data on a mini server in a consumer's home. Ray made an exceptional software system on the miscalculated premise that consumers would begin to buy their own memory storage servers for use in their own homes, which would lead to adoption of his software by the end consumer. He offered the software as a service (SaaS) through a paid subscription program, which could be downloaded from his website. Customers would then install the software on their own computers.

In hindsight, he was way too early with his SaaS offering. This was before there were any application stores on smartphones. Self-Server needed distribution through an application store on a device, but Apple's App Store wasn't even released until summer 2008. Ray's offering of Self-Server through a downloadable program on his website did not meet success. Less than five hundred downloads were registered, and the software was not regularly utilized.

Meanwhile, in the months and years to follow, cloud computing would become a ubiquitous term and the idea of having small in-home servers proved to be a failed idea. However, the underpinning technology of Self-Server became incredibly important to cloud computing. Underfunded, Self-Server was leapfrogged quickly by several cloud companies, and Self-Server realized it had to pivot its strategy.

In 2013, Ray came to my team in Chicago and asked if we could value his patent portfolio and accompanying IP technology, which was only a few years old. He had no evidence of use (EoU), but he was certain many companies were using his technology. The second part of the AIA's PTAB process was going into effect in the coming months, but we had no real way to assess the impact of the PTAB on Ray's patents. Ray's patent had won an award for innovation from the local chamber of commerce, and the Associated Press wire had picked up the story. Things in the industry were moving in the right direction for Ray; however, despite the accolades, Ray's company was not generating revenue.

Our IP valuation team reviewed his patent and software demonstrations. Clearly, the system had value in a business-to-business (B2B) setting. Ray had already been planning a pivot in his business to enterprise adoption. By 2015, Self-Server had conducted software demonstration meetings with IBM, EMC, Amazon, Oracle, HP, Google, and other companies.

The road show was exhausting, as Ray and his FIL went from office to office throughout the country. Many turned him down, but a few recognized the potential of Ray's software, and several gave long considerations for contractual business after meetings and demos. By the end of the road show, Self-Server signed an exclusive five-year, $25 million contract to deploy its software inside a Fortune 100 tech company.

By April 2014, Self-Server was up and running inside its clients' newly built data centers for the "cloud." Although the client was building data centers throughout the world, Self-Server was initially limited to operating in locations in the southwest of the US and for internal purposes only. While the software was eventually deployed globally, it was only ever used internally. Self-Server grew to about twelve employees with the initial client, with three employees focusing on finding new customers, while the other nine worked for the client as subcontractors.

Over the next five years, Self-Server was often asked to bring "all hands on deck" to solve software programming problems, and it hampered Self-Server's ability to find new customers. Sadly, Self-Server could never land new enterprise customers beyond its initial client. During the same time, the client made several multibillion-dollar acquisitions of companies operating in the same space as Self-Server. By the end of 2016, it was clear that Self-

Server's contract would not be renewed in favor of the competing product acquired through mergers and acquisitions (M&A).

What is worse, Ray realized that by working closely with their client, the client had copies of his original patented source code. He would need to document all the times and locations that his client had taken his code and deployed it elsewhere without permission. From what he and his programming team could tell, his source code worked better than the source code his client paid billions for through acquisition. Ray and his company would need to pivot their business once again or sell its software and IP to a third party. Figuring out how to sell their IP was not going to be easy.

EXPOSURE TO THE THIRD-PARTY PATENT STACK

Nearly every operating company valued greater than $20 billion in market capitalization is likely to be accused of patent infringement at some point. The high likelihood of utilizing another person's or company's patented technology led to an explosion of patent litigation activity over the last thirty years. Often, inventions emerge without a specific product in mind, and the strategy for the invention-turned-patent lacks a clear vision. This has been the way of invention since the patent offices were first formed and legal IP protection became a constitutionally ordained government program.

Nevertheless, invention is associated with the light bulb, Thomas Edison's iconic vision of a new idea. When the "light bulb" goes on, creative ingenuity brings a new way of doing things, and a patent is a way to secure a financial profit on that idea, provided the Inventor knows how to commercialize the invention. Invention is one side of the coin.

On the other side of the coin are Implementers who build

commercialized products. Expertise in commercialization is a uniquely different skill set from invention because business building requires interpersonal skills that are not always aligned with inventive skills. Said differently, Inventors are not always good at product development. As a result, Implementers with execution skills are known to push the boundaries of ethical in-licensing of others' IP. Moreover, consumers and buyers are usually less worried or concerned with fakes, frauds, or infringement, particularly if it is patent infringement. The operational decision to sell products infringing on IP is a choice made by an Implementer, and one that is policed only by the patent owner.

Figure 5: Two-sided coin of Invention and Implementer

Implementers who execute business morally and ethically will launch new products with a freedom to operate (FTO) study completed before the launch of the new product. The FTO will indicate where patented technology exists within a product, allowing the company to determine how to deal with the third-party patented technology in its product. For patented technology identified in the FTO study, the implementing company could in-license the patented technology or design a work-around. Sometimes, patented technology in a product is indemnified through supplier parts and agreements, and a license is provided as part of the indemnification. Finally, and most importantly, the FTO will indicate the Implementers' own patented technology used in its products and services. The full stack of technology in a product or service is categorized as follows:

Technology Stack in an Implementer's Product or Service

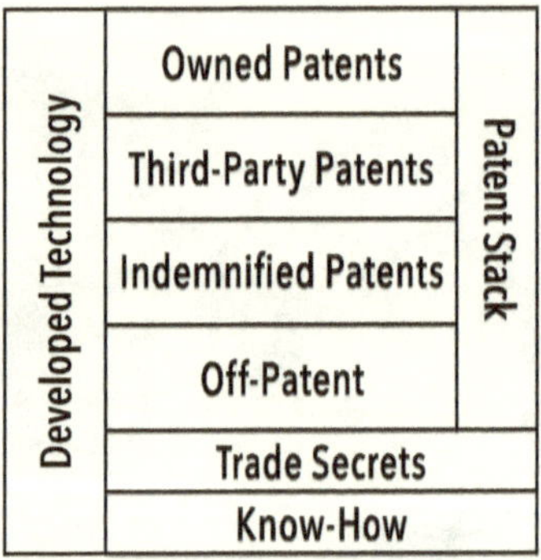

Figure 6: The Developed Technology Stack

The combination of patented technology in a product is called the "patent stack," which is a subset of the total technology stack. A technology stack is like an ingredient list of technology, IP, and patents in a product. The stack of patents is typically combined with technology enablement, such as trade secrets and know-how. The combination of patents, trade secrets, and know-how from employees creates the intangible asset of Developed Technology, an accounting term.

However, invention is often completed simultaneously by

competing groups. It is an inescapable fact. One that plagued Nathan Myhrvold, former Microsoft IP Chief Technology Officer and founder of Intellectual Ventures. During his early days at Microsoft, Nathan's role included responding to patent holders' requests for licenses. His issues at the time grew larger, and he is quoted in the book *Burning the Ships*:

> But Myhrvold soon realized just how deep Microsoft's patent deficit actually was. "As Microsoft got bigger," he explains, "all sorts of companies started coming around to see us. They'd claim that we were infringing their patents, and demand that we take a license. And I was like, 'Oh my God, they can do this? They can just demand money from us?' A lot of people were shocked by that, I can tell you. And when our lawyers looked around and asked what sort of patents we could assert back against these companies—in a sort of 'mutual assured destruction' show-down that would enable us to cross-license without having to fork over a lot of money—the answer was, 'We don't have crap.' So every time one of these companies came by to assert their patents against us, it would cost us money. Sometimes 50 or 100 million dollars. And that's a lot of zeroes to give away just because someone else has patents and you don't."

Nathan's dawning realization of vast infringement at Microsoft was not isolated to Microsoft. Throughout the 2000s, Big Tech companies have had a deficit of patented technology covering their products. The technological explosion that accompanied the birth of the internet led to an unprecedented number of patents being applied for and granted. With patent issuance on the rise, companies big and small were getting sued for patent infringement during the late '90s and early 2000s.

For Implementers being accused of patent infringement, determining a patent work-around or suggesting that the patent was not novel or obvious was a large company's best defense. Implementers accused of infringement in the early 2000s would submit the asserted patent for a re-examination process that would invalidate patents, but that was too slow. With the litigation damages outcomes and the number of patent litigations filed reaching record levels, operating companies began fighting for legislative change. So, in 2007, Google and a subset of companies with large exposure to claims of patent infringement created a private and public lobbying agenda to weaken the US patent system. The efforts to reshape the American view of patents started with the following:

- Overt funding to groups like the Electronic Frontier Foundation (EFF), the License on Transfer (LOT) network, and Allied Security Trust (AST);
- funding of academic research to anti-patent causes using well-known and tenured professors like Mark Lemley of Stanford, Jorge Contreras of the University of Utah, and Colleen Chien of UC Berkeley Law (formerly UC Davis);
- enlisting help from venture capital funds whose portfolio companies were caught up in litigation to supply lobbying and anti-patent support to legislative change; and
- the many patent holders who could not help themselves with filing frivolous lawsuits that led to genuine abuse of the patent system.

As technology advances at a breakneck pace, lobbying efforts to change and slow the US patent system continue. Seeing that Barack Obama was on pace to win the US presidency in 2008, Google became very close with his administration. Big Tech's lobbying efforts, specifically Google's, advanced the calls for patent reform, and by 2011, the AIA was the law of the land.

Eventually, Michelle Lee, the former head of IP at Google, was called upon to be the USPTO's director from 2015 to 2017, where she oversaw the largest anti-patent movement in the US in modern times. Google's regulatory capture of the patent system has created an oligopoly in which a few large, dominant companies control vast swathes of technology commerce.

While the DOJ pursues antitrust justice, it has turned a blind eye to IP and patent infringement accusations that the same Big Tech companies it is investigating are allegedly committing with alarming frequency. Put differently, if a student had been accused of plagiarism on repeated occasions by numerous teachers, we would believe the teachers. In the same way, patent owners are credibly accusing Big Tech companies of infringement in courts throughout the country, and the outcomes have been getting staggeringly worse for patent holders.

Why is the intransigence toward third-party patents so high from Big Tech?

THE FINANCIAL EXPOSURE MODEL

Paying third-party patent licensing fees lowers earnings per share (EPS). It causes CFOs to lower earnings expectations to Wall Street financial analysts. It is an uncertain event that creates havoc for public companies that need certainty and sustainable revenue and profits. To that end, most Big Tech IP departments are tasked with figuring out how *not* to pay patent licensing fees. This makes for an incredibly tricky problem for alleged infringers. Implementers accused of infringement rely upon a wide variety of methods to undermine patent litigations.

Unfortunately for Implementers, patented inventions accumulate within an Implementer's product, creating products that incorporate hundreds, if not thousands, of patents. These patents are either owned or not owned by the implementing company, and understanding which patents are the ingredients that make up a product is defined through an FTO study. Once the FTO study is completed, determining a reasonable royalty for internally generated versus third-party licensing rates is possible. But how? More importantly, who would be willing to disclose such a figure?

The answer is recently acquired companies through corporate M&A. The financial reporting guidance requires companies to value their Developed Technology, and place the value on its balance sheet. This accounting rule was born out of a few notable events that uniquely shaped the IP valuation world:

1. The dot-com bubble popping from 2000 to 2002,
2. Enron's financial collapse in 2002, and
3. the failure of Arthur Andersen, one of the former Big 5 accounting firms.

Due to the financial disruptions from those events, which caused significant economic harm, Congress passed the most comprehensive regulatory accounting changes in decades, known as the Sarbanes-Oxley Act (SOX). SOX altered how companies account for acquired assets in M&A. The old and simplistic methods of "pool" accounting for combined companies were wildly inaccurate relative to the fair value of an acquired company's assets. When SOX became law in 2002, almost overnight, a nascent finance industry of business and intangible asset valuation practitioners emerged. I got swept up in these new business practices, and thus began in 2002 my career valuing IP and intangible assets.

Since then, I have been involved with tens of thousands of business and intangible asset valuations for every reason a person can think of. It often feels like I am a wizard conducting financial sorcery to determine the "fair value" of IP or intangible assets. There is a reason for this: IP valuation is a human algorithm that ties together a myriad of unlikely data and structures it into a financial estimate. Proving that value estimate is impractical in most instances because it is an IP asset. Accurate valuations have a strong tie to price, and IP does not have a meaningful transaction market by which to reconcile value versus price. Accordingly, debate and disagreement between reasonable people about the value of IP creates an underlying tension. The tension that exists when presenting IP asset value is a lack of credibility. Are you able to take the valuation estimate you just provided and turn it into a transactable price for the IP asset? Will the IP asset value hold up in a liquidation scenario? More often than not, the answer is no.

Valuing IP is not for the faint of heart. It is exceedingly difficult, and yet it is vitally important to IP owners. However, the AIA has made the value versus price of IP and patent assets nearly impossible to accurately calculate. Creating an active IP marketplace that includes disclosure of IP monetization transactions is a linchpin to accurately valuing IP. Without an active IP marketplace, it becomes exceedingly difficult to accurately value IP.

Fortunately, the change in leadership at the USPTO in 2025 has brought a new view toward patents that had previously been absent. Deputy Director Coke Morgan Stewart (formerly the interim acting director) and USPTO Director John Squires are actively limiting the impact of the PTAB's IPRs through discretionary denials. The actions to limit IPR proceedings have caused an uproar of anti-patent sentiment to come rushing into the conversation, in defense of patent invalidation proceedings. The fight over the entire patent system appears to be getting more contentious and heated.

Historically, the divide between IP licensees and IP licensors has been a torturous fight waged through the court systems, legislative changes, and regulatory lobbying. From 1982 through 2011, the Inventors were winning the battle thanks to years of outsized patent litigation damages outcomes. The strength of the US patent system gave patent holders the leverage to win patent litigation cases, until the Implementers could change the laws. Once that happened, the pendulum swung financially in favor of Implementers, leaving patent owners in the lurch. However, the legislative change that was meant to rein in patent trolls overcorrected, leaving legitimate patent holders with limited options for recourse when patent infringement is discovered.

The fight against patent trolls has always been built upon a faulty premise: that patents are a tax on innovation. Rather, patents should be considered the first "open source" technology transfer mechanism ever developed. If companies and enterprises considered the patent system as an extension of their R&D department, with an expectation of in-licensing third-party patents to save on in-house R&D expenses, a transactable market for patent licensing could more easily take shape. Instead, however, most operating companies have an insidious belief that technology "not invented here" should be denied. Not invented here is the ethos of all tech companies accused of patent infringement.

IP from a third party, and not paid for has become socially acceptable among the large company community. There is an ongoing endemic of unauthorized patent use, and the primary solution has always been patent litigation because paying licensing fees hurts large company investors. As a result, when patent reform legislation became a bipartisan opportunity in 2010, leading to the AIA, reform was embraced despite the solution being only half conceived as a legitimate solution for all inventive participants. Instead, Big Tech lobbyists took hold of the US legislature and pushed through patent reform that has taken the US patent system to its knees for a huge swath of Inventors. The overcorrection to the problem of patent trolls will make the US patent system irrelevant, if not fixed.

BUILDING THE FINANCIAL "EXPOSURE" MODEL

Patent hold-out explains what an Implementer does when a patent holder requests a license from the Implementer, and the Implementer delays or refuses to compensate the patent holder for unauthorized use. In most cases, the Implementer can continue selling its alleged infringing product, but holds out from paying licensing fees until compelled to do so through the court system. Oftentimes, an Implementer that loses a patent litigation can continue to delay paying patent fees through the entire appeal process through the Federal Circuit. As an Implementer, holding out is the prudent course of action and is in the best interests of the Implementer's investors.

The world's most famous Implementers are the "Magnificent Seven." These companies, whose market capitalization has exceeded $1 trillion (as of this writing), include Amazon, Apple, Alphabet (Google), Meta (Facebook), Microsoft, NVIDIA, and Tesla. These seven companies represent the world's largest collection of "alleged" patent infringers.

The Magnificent Seven has incredible exposure to patent litigation, with over 3,670 patent litigations filed against the seven. Unsurprisingly, the Magnificent Seven were the biggest beneficiaries of the efforts to enact the AIA. As a result, the Magnificent Seven are leaders of invalidating third-party patents. Here is a summary related to patent litigation from RPX Insights as of year-end 2023:

Magnificent Seven Total Patent Litigation Summary in 2023

Patent Litigation Summary	Total	Active	IPR Petitions	Patent Defend	Patent Plaintiff
Amazon	710	49	159	692	18
Apple	1,112	71	981	1,004	108
Google (Alphabet)	769	68	642	734	35
Meta (Facebook)	230	15	215	212	18
Microsoft	980	35	381	865	115
NVIDIA	124	0	43	118	6
Tesla	49	13	26	46	3
TOTAL	3,974	251	2,447	3,671	303

Figure 7

While the number of patent assertions against the Magnificent Seven is staggering, so too are the revenue figures of the combined seven at $1.8 trillion in 2024. Amazingly, revenue for the Magnificent Seven is estimated to grow to $3.5 trillion by 2030. With that much control of the US and global economy in seven companies, it stands to reason that they would uphold the highest ethical standards regarding utilizing other entities' patented technology, but the numbers tell the actual story.

The Magnificent Seven companies are defendants in hundreds of active patent litigation cases. In a direct correlation, the same seven companies actively work to invalidate the patents asserted against them, highlighting their attempt to kill (and thus avoid paying for) other Inventors' work. But why do these companies fight so hard to protect their Developed Technology while invalidating another person's patents? The simple answer is profits. Not paying patent licensing fees improves profitability; therefore, they do everything possible not to pay patent licensing fees.

So, how much are the Magnificent Seven saving by acting

obstinately about paying third-party patent licenses? I have made an estimate using a simplistic formula and then back-solved to ensure the outcomes were reasonable.

How to determine patented IP liability is based on revenues or a royalty base that is subject to using third-party patents, resulting in licensing fees that should be paid. For the Magnificent Seven, revenues are publicly known through SEC filings (i.e., 10-Qs and 10-Ks), which show the latest twelve months of revenues for the Magnificent Seven in 2024 on the chart below.

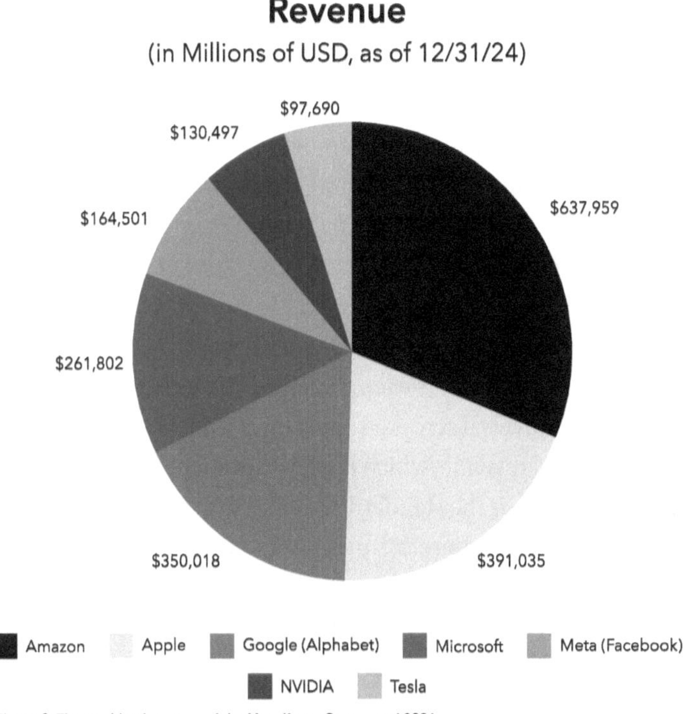

Figure 8: The combined revenue of the Magnificent Seven as of 2024

Using the public revenue of the Magnificent Seven and building the forecast financial data as provided by New York University corporate finance professor Aswath Damodaran, I created "top-down" licensing models for each individual Magnificent Seven company. The models from Damodaran's blog provide forecast revenue growth estimates, which can be used to create a simple licensing fee model that would mimic a hypothetical situation where each individual Magnificent Seven company would pay patent licensing fees in line with their "alleged" infringement.

In the most simplistic terms, a tiny sliver of a royalty rate can be carved out of the revenues, and allocated to the varied entities accusing the Magnificent Seven of patent infringement. At even the most conservative of estimates, paying royalties of 0.1 percent to 0.2 percent on revenues will result in billions of patent licensing fees paid to third-party patent owners. Of course, the actual royalty rates will vary on a case-by-case basis, but for simplicity, these estimates explain why the fight over patents is so significant.

Implementers carry an extraordinary level of patent liability when reduced to licensing fees paid to third parties. These liabilities are why large Implementers have worked covertly in the undermining of the IP system. Further, the exposure to patent liabilities is universal across all companies with more than $20 billion in annual revenue, which is why intransigence toward other people's patents is the standard response from all Implementers.

In a scenario where 0.2 percent of all revenues represent the Magnificent Seven's patent liability annually, the patent licensing fees would be billions annually. Those patent licensing fees would unquestionably lower EPS in big companies and the investment managers would be forced to look for financial returns elsewhere. As a result, the entire financial system is happy to allow the regulatory capture of the patent system, which allows the Magnificent Seven to inflate its earnings by underpaying patent licensing fees.

Inflated earnings have been built on large companies' inaccurate belief that everything they sell has implicit freedom to operate (FTO) because it has been invented in-house. This false notion makes large companies unwilling to pay licensing fees to third-party patented technology. Instead, they leaned into the patent troll narrative of boogeyman Inventors sent to destroy operating companies. By labeling *all* enforcing patent owners as trolls regardless of the facts, the Magnificent Seven has created an environment where not paying patent licensing fees has resulted in outsized returns. The chasm that has resulted between Inventors and Implementers is gigantic, and it seems unlikely that a bridge to connect them is possible without significant intervention from the government.

For the Magnificent Seven, saying no to requests for a patent license is a source of pride for many in-house IP attorneys. At one of the Magnificent Seven, the in-house IP acquisition attorney told me he was quite happy to report that they had not bought any patents for the last two years despite having a never-ending supply of offerings.

And that is where the problem lies: The USPTO is issuing patents that are not licensable to potential would-be buyers or licensees that use the patented technology of third parties. While there are currently around 3.5 million active US patents, experts suggest that only 35,000 to 350,000 of those patents are actively being used in commercialized products. That means nearly 90 percent of all patents issued never turn into a commercialized product, and the USPTO is issuing millions of worthless patents.

In the exceedingly rare times when a patent holder believes he is being infringed, the alleged infringer uses the following defense:

That patent should never have been issued in the first place.

The threat of invalidation places incredible pressure on good patent holders with credible claims of infringement. It is victim blaming at its highest level, and petitioning patents for IPR is part of the corporate playbook anytime a patent holder asserts their rights against alleged infringers. Who could blame them, as invalidation removes potential infringement liability? It does not make economic sense to pay licensing fees when invalidating delays payment, and petitioning for a patent invalidation is so easy. The AIA has made it easy to be a serial infringer.

THE CYCLE OF DENIAL ENRICHMENT

Large companies have made great investments over the last fifteen years. For Big Tech companies, a strong stream of cash flow and profitability has led to record market values. The cycle has increased virtuously, and the larger a company's market value, the higher the cash flows. The CEOs of large companies have figured out how to position themselves quarterly and annually to not shock Wall Street estimates, creating a predictable market for professional investors.

As the financial markets have shifted toward more automated trading platforms, large companies have become increasingly robotic in their approach to quarterly earnings calls, seeking to align their financial expectations with those of Wall Street analysts. Occasionally, an earnings surprise for large companies will send a shock through a stock or an industry, moving it up or down dramatically (e.g., the Lyft typo's impact on its stock price is an example). However, shortly after the surprise, the stock will resettle at its new level and the company's revenue and earnings reporting will resume as normal.

Imagine, however, that large companies start paying patent licensing fees. The CFO's guidance on earnings would likely move down across many quarters, causing a sustained drop in EPS. Reduced profitability is a fundamental reason large companies deny patent infringement accusations. They are incentivized to deny it because large companies might begin to see a steadier stream of outbound licensing agreements, resulting in long-term lowered earnings. This would break the cycle of denial, resulting in systemic change for most companies. As a result, the cycle of denial must stay intact.

When public companies release their quarterly earnings, AI algorithm trading programs use the information to enact trading strategies that align with the results. Accordingly, the predictability of quarterly earnings reports becomes critically important to the trading machines that make the financial markets work. Paying third-party patent licensing fees is disruptive to those orchestrated earnings outcomes, so denying and not paying patent licensing fees becomes commonplace, particularly when the Magnificent Seven are the leaders of not paying patent and IP licensing fees to third parties. "If they're not paying, why should we pay?" is a common (unspoken) belief among the large companies.

As a result, companies have an (unstated) obligation to their investors to deny paying third-party patent and IP licensing requests indefinitely. Most large companies follow their own version of the unwritten playbook of denial and delay, and with patents having only a twenty-year lifespan (or less if not utilized), it is easy to run out the clock before paying a patent licensing cent—the process of the cycle of denial enrichment.

As an initial start, the base action is to not pay patent or IP licensing fees from third parties. Of course, many large companies claim they pay IP licensing fees, but I would estimate that more than 90 percent of those patent license fees are based on evidence of use (EoU) claim charts. With those EoUs, the companies would be subjected to patent litigation, but for the ability to delay and deny.

There are always many company-to-company patent and IP licensing deals. Ericsson, Nokia, Sisvel, Broadcom, Intel, and others often announce large nine-figure licensing deals for a term of six or seven years. Industry watchers applaud these licensing deals as a success of the patent industry to cohesively work together. But those are just the headlines. Below the surface, where the reporting goes less often, are the smaller and individual Inventors getting steamrolled by the cycle of denial enrichment.

The Cycle of Denial Enrichment

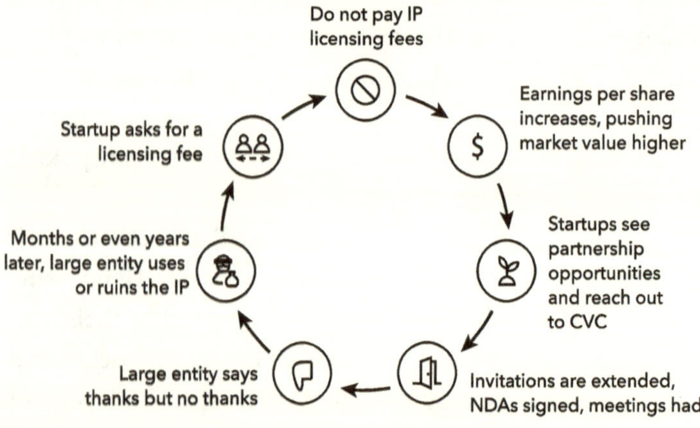

Figure 9

After a large public company denies paying licensing fees, it will maintain or improve its EPS, pushing its market value higher. Improving market value acts as a beacon signal of growth and profitability. Since early-stage, inventive companies are looking for fast scaling to get adoption of their technology, early-stage inventive tech companies will seek partnerships with corporate CVC investors. Almost every company worth more than $100 billion has a CVC or invests in a group CVC. The investment statistics and outcomes for CVCs are varied and difficult to benchmark, but the model's internal rate of return (IRR) is determined based on the success of between 1 percent to 5 percent of VC's investment outcomes being home runs. Since VC success rates are low, the CVCs can operate as a strategic VC investor while subversively being a ruse to gather strategic information. CVC arms invite early-stage companies into their posh headquarters in Silicon Valley or the Northwest and they entice them with investment, which brings down the startup's guard.

After nondisclosure agreements (NDAs) are signed and the conversations are going well, the larger company will invite the startup's product development team for technical discussions. The large company will bring five people to one for the startup, making for a twenty-five- to thirty-five-person room. The meeting will last hours or even days, with detailed technical discussions that eventually lead to confirming ideas or technical specifications for the large company's R&D team. Some people would say that technical data trade secrets are being transferred to the large CVC team unwittingly. The meetings will end with thanks and praise. And promises for callbacks. Then, the startup company's CEO and technical teams will wait anxiously for the callback. Days will turn into weeks. Weeks into months, and then the email: "Thanks, but no thanks."

Because startup companies are ambitious, competitive, and focused, they move on to the next opportunity for investment and growth, rather than explore a potential IP infringement scenario. Entrepreneurs and founders who are in the high-growth game follow the VC growth path, expecting them to be building a user base followed by annualized recurring revenue or ARR. This type of fast-paced growth requires chasing VC at regular intervals, resulting in round after round of VC series funding. Entrepreneurs who play this game with VCs will downplay their Inventor side so as not to pick fights about patents.

However, literally every Inventor I have ever met, thousands of them at this point, does not want patent litigation to be their primary source of income. That includes the so-called patent maximalists or patent trolls. Patent litigation is extremely stressful, and high risk. Moreover, under the current patent laws, patent litigation primarily benefits two parties: the lawyers and the infringers. Are there Inventors who just want to litigate? Not like there used to be. These days, most Inventors have hopeful yet dogmatic notions of licensing IP to a large company without a fight. Unfortunately, those situations are rare.

Eventually, some months or years later, the startup's IP will show up in the same large company's product. Or the company will take the trade secrets and publish them in a patent application, which happened in *Masimo v. Apple*. If the startup catches the large company in the act of infringement, the startup should have an opportunity to address the infringement in court and get a settlement or investment. Not anymore. Now, companies that find out a large company is infringing its patents need to litigate to receive restitution. And the restitution is always below what the patent holder believes is fair value. More likely, however, is that the patent holder loses the patent in an IPR process, a devastating blow for an Inventor's patent to be reversed in such a manner.

Given the relative ease of large corporations delaying and not paying, most companies deploy the cycle of denial enrichment as the (unwritten) standard operating procedure. Add the fact that US patent invalidation rates were above 80 percent when instituted, and the risk of invalidation casts a pall on the entire patent system in the US. The legal stranglehold by which the PTAB shrouds the patent system ultimately smothers smaller and individual patent holders from making reasonable decisions.

To break the cycle of denial enrichment, a (compulsory) willingness of Implementers to disclose adopted and integrated technology is necessary for change. Transparency in the right ways is a critical linchpin in transitioning IP into a platform that is monetizable.

In doing this, however, a great issue becomes exposed: I estimate the financial liability to third-party patent owners by the Magnificent Seven to be $16.7 billion to $33.5 billion in potential value lost that should be transferred to patent owners over the next eight years.

That is a staggering figure, and is based solely on 0.1 percent to 0.2 percent of revenue. By denying the payment of patent licensing fees, value accrues to the Magnificent Seven through "trickle-up" economics.

This is the most concrete evidence that the playing field is uneven and tilted in favor of Big Tech.

CHAPTER 4

REDISCOVERING IP CAPITAL

"So if you ask me what the single lesson I learned was, liquidity equals value. You have no value if you have no liquidity."

—SAM ZELL, LIFELONG BUSINESSMAN AND INVESTOR

PIVOT! RECOVERING LOST INVESTMENT THROUGH PATENTS

In the spring of 2017, during my first year at Houlihan Lokey, Ray, his FIL, and his brother-in-law (BIL) requested an updated valuation of their patent portfolio. Ray and Self-Server had managed to pivot and deploy the software into a Fortune 100 tech company for internal use on every continent except Antarctica. Ray was halfway through fulfilling his contract. The company had success, but the next customer was elusive, and their one client was going through a management change. Things were evolving, and Ray needed strategic options.

Ray had built a meaningful SaaS system with an API and an SDK. Moreover, the patent had become foundational to cloud companies' operating data centers. Securely storing data and information has become increasingly more expensive due to the costs of transporting information over a network. Ray's SaaS helped to reduce the need for computational output to back up files across various servers, and his invention was being emulated around the world.

The wrinkle they were not expecting was that everything about the patent system had been flipped upside down since 2013. By 2017, we understood the impact the PTAB had on patent portfolios, and the entire, previously completed IP and patent valuation process needed to be updated. As we updated the valuation of Ray's patents, two things became clear:

1. Ray's patent carried the risk of invalidation, and
2. there was vast unauthorized use by multiple companies in the cloud and data center space.

Some of the allegedly infringing companies had extremely deep pockets, and there was a "long tail" of potential infringers at lower revenue levels using Ray's patents. It was clear that Ray's patent was critical to the cloud, but to receive his due compensation for unauthorized use, Ray would need to fight back against efforts to invalidate his patents.

It was a terrible position to be in. The broad use of Ray's patents by third-party SaaS cloud companies was becoming increasingly brazen. If Ray were to pursue the infringers, the effort to invalidate his patents would rise significantly. The fight against the alleged infringers for unauthorized use had become exceedingly difficult, so Ray hoped there would be a buyer for his patents. We formulated a plan to sell Ray's patents, but it would be risky. The reliability of the patent system under the AIA had become suspect. Without reliable rights associated with patents, the sale process would be like skating across thin ice.

Despite having a novel and original design for SaaS, the patent system was failing Ray. If Ray wanted to receive full value for his IP, he was in for the fight of his life. However, Ray was not keen on having the fight of his life. He wanted to sell. He had spent the last ten years building a business, and it had not gone as he had wanted or expected. He had been both wildly successful and on the verge of failure within a twelve-year window.

IMPLEMENTERS VS. INVENTORS

Invention is the birth of innovation. It is an act of creation in and of itself, but it is often subsumed into the separate creation of a business enterprise. Technology and business creation are not the same thing, but as a society, we equate the two things with the idea that patented technology will help launch a business. However, many Inventors are just that: Inventors. Bringing the invention they have created from their minds does not qualify them as the businessperson who brings an invented product to life.

At the seed level, startup company failure rates typically approach 75 percent to 90 percent. For inventive startups with patents, their creations are public ideas that solve problems in a new way, and unrelated Implementers often take and use those inventions, wittingly or unwittingly, to the detriment of the Inventor. History is littered with Inventors who fail to commercialize meaningfully. As such, inventorship can be a tortured profession of creation followed by watching others become rich. While some Inventors, like Benjamin Franklin, believed in freely giving inventions away for the greater good, others, like Nikola Tesla, were tormented by the commercialization process of their inventions.

Implementers of commercialized products are renowned for skimming inventions from others into their own products. They are usually businesspeople who understand the business of building companies through manufacturing, distribution, marketing, and scaling. For Implementers, invention is only a small aspect of a broader set of circumstances that create wealth. For Implementers, coming in second place in the invention can often provide unique leverage against the patented Inventor, if the business aspects of implementation are already in place. It is why so many companies are accused of infringing patented technology, and those accusations have not abated since the AIA became law, which is curious since the AIA was meant to reduce patent litigation. Clearly, the AIA is not working as it was intended.

In rare exceptions, the Inventor and Implementer are the same person, and they become wildly successful. These are the rock stars of industry. Elon Musk, Steve Jobs, Bill Gates, Sergey Brin, and Mark Zuckerberg are iconic Inventors who have built the world's largest companies based on their initial inventions that became groundbreaking companies. Ironically, the iconic inventions of businesspeople usually fade into the background, and their newfound wealth allows them to hire the best and the brightest people imaginable. Empires are built, and moats to protect the products they sell enable their companies to stay ahead of the little guy in his garage trying to disrupt them. The result is that society's earliest disruptive heroes, such as Google, Apple, Facebook, or Amazon, often become patent pariahs once they make it big, and they stealthily adopt other Inventors' technology and then "leave lawyers to sort it."

In the late 1990s, when the technological waves of disruption came with the deployment of the internet and wireless connectivity, patent applications and issuance grew in correlation with the new technology deployed. Because invention is often a race, simultaneous invention is commonplace, and the USPTO is left to sort it out. Unfortunately, the USPTO was ill-equipped to handle the nonstop technological progress that led to continuous, record patent applications.

The US patent system can barely keep up with the application process, yet the arcane manner of applying for patents and issuing them, as well as the pendency time for issuing patents, continues to get longer and longer. Long-term pendency times harm the entire system. Technology has moved too fast for the USPTO to keep up, and because the race to innovate moves so quickly, the likelihood of infringement by Implementers has become nearly commonplace for most companies. Rather than admit unauthorized use, and pay a reasonable royalty, intransigence against all patents is a common refrain from Implementers.

IP CAPITAL

Intellectual property capital is an investment secured by legally protected IP assets and the underlying intangible assets that support it. When Investors think of investment capital, they think of two main vehicles: debt or equity. Similarly, IP capital can take a similar form where lending (IP debt) or ownership (IP equity) is the form of investment backed by IP assets that generate cash flows. The cash flow from IP can then be allocated to the corresponding type of IP capital.

IP debt is a less risky form of IP capital than IP equity. Terms for IP debt would be similar to typical debt, except rather than payments via interest, its payment would be through royalties on sales (or another royalty base), all other terms being equal. IP debt is an ideal investment structure for early-stage companies that prefer avoiding equity dilution and have limited other assets for collateral purposes.

From an Investor perspective, IP debt provides earliest-stage investors with an opportunity to place a security interest lien on IP, particularly patents (or other legally protected IP in the walls of the IP Pyramid Fortress). Security interest liens are only available on legally protected assets under the Uniform Commercial Code (UCC), Article 9, on secure transactions. To fully leverage the intangible asset of Developed Technology for IP Capital, a bridge between the UCC and the accounting term needs to be connected by regulators and auditors to enable an IP Capital system.

Developed Technology is the financial accounting term used during the creation of SOX legislation that enacted the accounting of intangible assets on a balance sheet. Developed Technology exists at many companies, but the narrow and limited accounting guidance only allows for Developed Technology to be placed on a balance sheet after an M&A. This accounting procedure operates as an encumbrance on the IP asset's ownership because it is not recognized at its earliest creation and placed on a balance sheet. Said differently, the SOX accounting regulations have operated as a half-baked legislative cake for intangible assets for over two decades.

The accounting guidance related to intangible assets that emerged from SOX created a means by which intangible assets can and should be accounted for. However, after its implementation into the accounting system, it has been relegated to a compliance-driven activity that provides limited value to Investors. Nevertheless, after SOX became a law in the US, the International Financial Reporting Standards (IFRS) created similar rules related to recognizing intangible assets, but again, only after an M&A.

Absent from US GAAP is the accounting of "internally generated intangible assets." While IFRS has rules related to accounting for internally generated intangible assets, it is reduced to a "cost approach" measure of value only. Practically, the cost approach to IP assets often undervalues the income potential gained by owning the IP assets. As a result, the accounting for intangible assets is inaccurate in reflecting the true value of these assets because the procedures do not accurately represent market value. This creates a "chicken or egg" problem for accounting for intangible assets. Early-stage companies with exceptional IP but limited market traction can often see their IP vanish, only to reappear in a larger competitor's products.

On the other hand, for large companies, a semi-complete understanding of incorporated Developed Technology into a product or service creates unaccounted-for intangible asset liabilities. These IP liabilities should be budgeted for, and a large company's IP group should in-license the IP in good faith. However, most IP groups at large companies are tasked with saying no to as many requests for a license as possible.

It does not have to be this way.

For commercialized products and services, a portion of operating margin can be attributed to the patented technology in the product. That portion of operating margin can be bifurcated into two segments:

1. Internally generated IP income that can be financialized into IP capital securities
2. Licensing fees owed to a third party for use

Recognizing the cash flow from a product that can be allocated between internally generated IP and third-party IP is an action that has been grossly ignored since the dawn of business enterprises. It is a concept that should be simple to understand, but it is ignored because of the impact on operating margins. Recognizing the difference, however, is the beginning of transformative change for startup companies looking to leverage their IP into investment capital.

IP capital is not the panacea to all the patent industry woes, but it is the start of a transformation in how early-stage companies can attract investment, and how large companies can create legitimate freedom to operate. The Developed Technology that can be attributed to a product or service can be classified into three primary groups, as follows:

1. Patents
2. Trade secrets
3. Know-how

Patented technology in a product falls into a series of subcategories, including:

1. Owned patents
2. Indemnified patents
3. Third-party patents
4. Off-patent or expired

Once a hierarchy of technology deployed into a product is established, the IP technology can then be attributed to a self-declared royalty rate on the product or service. The following table provides an illustrative example of how it could work:

Product Technology Stack Allocated to a Royalty Rate

Developed Technology		IP Royalty	Royalty Rate (RR)	RR Allocation	IP Rate by Tech
Owned Patents	Patent Stack	Saved	7%	20%	1.4%
Third-Party Patents		Owed		10%	0.7%
Indemnified Patents		Saved		0%	0%
Off-Patent		Saved		0%	0%
Trade Secrets		Saved		30%	2.1%
Know-How		Saved		40%	2.8%
	TOTAL		7%	100%	7.0%

Figure 10: Connecting the Technology Stack to the Royalty Stack

By declaring a royalty rate for a product or service, the technology stack can be allocated to the underlying type of technology that is included in the product. By the Implementer declaring the royalty rate, the bid-ask spread from Inventor to Implementer becomes conjoined. Absent the product's declared royalty rate, the Implementer and the Inventor are negotiating a royalty rate from two different places where agreement is nearly impossible because there is no transparency or pricing discovery that can bridge the gap to make an agreement. However, suppose the Implementer has declared a royalty for the product. In that case, the technical stack and royalty stack can be allocated to the underlying income generated by the IP, and an explicit IP value can be determined.

ROYALTY RATES FOR IP TECHNOLOGY

IP technology royalty rates have been built upon a house of cards over the last forty years. In the absence of pricing disclosure requirements, IP market participants are left to determine IP royalty rates based on the agreements of parties willing to disclose their rates. These brave souls who have made public their IP licensing rates have created a market for IP licensing despite the inherent bias that exists by selecting only the rates that are willfully disclosed.

There are a handful of IP royalty rate service providers, including ktMine, RoyaltySource, RoyaltyStat, and IntangibleSpring. These service providers have been accumulating IP licensing agreements for benchmarking purposes that are then repackaged and sold to a variety of professional service providers, completing compliance-driven work for accounting and tax.

While these royalty rate service providers work hard aggregating IP licensing rates, the information they collect is used to inform the valuation of tens of thousands of intangible assets that have been acquired via M&A. In addition, the IP licensing rates are used to inform the intercompany transfer pricing rates for literally millions of MNE internal IP agreements that seek to optimize their effective tax rates across their global operations.

Licensing Agreements
(Public vs. Private)

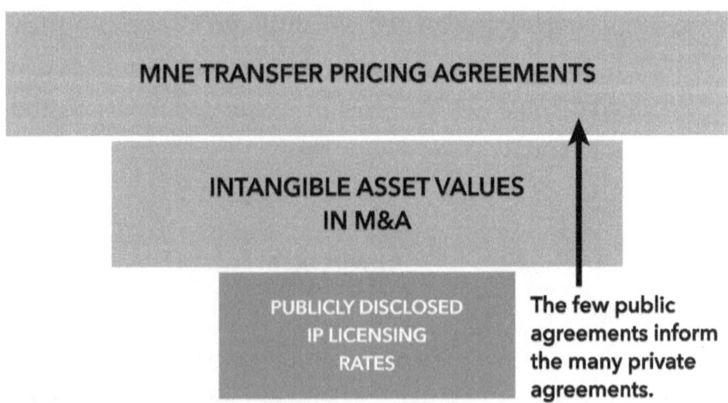

Figure 11: Public vs. Private Licensing Agreements

The inverted dynamic of public information supporting private intercompany transactions is a major source of support in the "optimization of tax expenses" on a global level (also known as transfer pricing). Thanks to this globally accepted arrangement by the various taxing authorities, internally generated IP assets have become extraordinarily valuable, enabling profit shifting to occur with ease to the detriment of taxing collecting authorities across the globe, but I digress. More on the practice of transfer pricing will be discussed in Chapter 8.

Despite the logical fallacy of undisclosed royalty rates, if Implementers started declaring their own royalty rate for Developed Technology, a solution to the problem of serial efficient infringement takes shape. Requiring transparency and public disclosure of freedom to operate (FTO) studies would be a major advancement. For individual and small Inventors that regularly find infringement by Big Tech, creating a framework for easily licensing patents rather than invalidation is a systematic change that would defuse capital more broadly throughout the economy.

Of course, there is no imaginable way that Big Tech companies would willingly make public their FTO studies. The liability would be too large, maybe 0.1 percent to 0.2 percent of total revenue (maybe more). So as long as Inventors believe that Implementers are using their patented technology without authorization, the patent fights and litigation will continue. While the AIA was meant to limit litigation, its outcome has been far harsher toward Inventors than Implementers. And now that Implementers are accustomed to the profit margin associated with taking patented technology for free, the willingness to give up licensing fees for another's patent technology is completely absent from the minds of C-suite executives at large companies.

Having dealt with and spoken to countless corporate IP departments about the value of their patent portfolios, the internal silos that exist between IP, accounting/finance, and product development are too stark to consider the technology IP accounted for in a product holistically. As a result, IP value becomes a fungible figure depending on the purpose, to the point where accounting books and tax books are separately filed in MNEs. It creates incentives to distort internally generated IP values, and it is so ingrained in MNE tax-paying operations, it undermines the attempted creations of a patent and IP marketplace.

However, there is a group of businesses where invention and implementation are the same: pre-revenue companies raising angel to Series A funding rounds. These companies are often the most inventive but have trouble commercializing for many reasons. In fact, the failure rate for companies between angel and Series A is in the thousands of companies every year. In startup terms, these failures come in the "Startup Death Valley" between proof of concept and scaling.

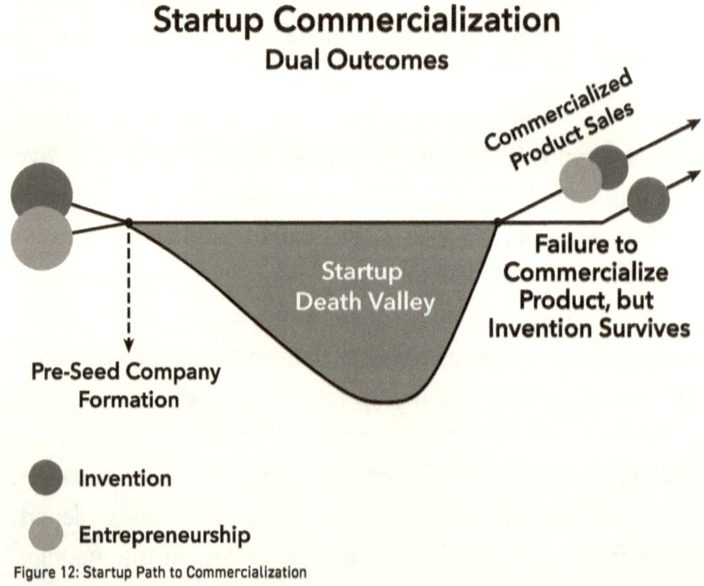

Figure 12: Startup Path to Commercialization

For most of these early-stage companies, the reasons for the failure are as varied as the founders who started them. A confluence of factors is likely contributing to the failures of companies that cannot make it to a Series A funding round, but unquestionably, the common failure is a lack of revenue. It is the trait that explains why so many companies die in the Startup Death Valley. It is with revenue scaling that IP and intangible assets become real, and not just an option or abstract idea. Startup values soar once revenue becomes consistent. The value of startup companies from Series A to B to C increases by orders of magnitude because of revenue growth.

A more apt analogy is to consider a seed-level startup company to be a rocket, sitting on its launch pad. Investment is its fuel and revenue is the reward. Most of these rockets fail to launch, and most founders will say, "If only I had the investment, I'd be able to take off." For the few that do take off, the startups become the stars in our eyes, and the companies are heralded. However, most startups fail, usually crashing and burning. As an IP appraiser, I am often called in to help salvage the wreckage: Is the IP worth anything now that the startup has failed?

The short answer is: not likely. IP from a bankrupt startup has value in limited cases, and when it does, it is reported in the news. When it does not, the value is absorbed into the ethos of other businesses, particularly other Implementers, and the IP becomes freely available to the market. At that point, investment recovery becomes extremely difficult.

Over the years, holding infringers responsible for unauthorized use has gone from difficult to nearly impossible. The onus is on a patent holder to prove the Implementer uses the patented technology. This proof comes from an analysis called an evidence of use (EoU) chart, which matches the claims of a patent to the technology of a product or service. Inside the R&D groups at large corporate entities, engineers work diligently to design work-arounds for patents from third parties. Moreover, creating EoUs is an inexact science that relies on publicly disclosed information, and large entities conceal most technical information, making the creation of an EoU harder than ever.

With a weakened patent system, Implementers are engaging in more patent infringement than ever. Before the AIA, patents that would have won large damages awards are now being invalidated. The PTAB has lowered the standards for disqualifying patented inventions in post-grant procedural proceedings, creating a recession and now depression for the patent market. With IPR risk being so high, large companies accused of patent infringement often gain their FTO at the expense of small, inventive companies that lack the same resources as big companies.

Ultimately, what should be a symbiotic relationship between Inventors and corporations has become parasitic. For Inventors, their diminished role and importance within the broader economy hurts innovation. Inventors are vital creators, and the continued effort to undermine their role has been devastating. The outsized growth and power of fast-growing entrepreneurs and corporations have fundamentally created an imbalance in the system. It was not always like this in the early stages of invention and entrepreneurship, and it is my hope that a restoration toward a more balanced approach can be created, through the financialization of patented IP.

THE INTERSECTION OF IP AND FINANCE: ROYALTY RATES VS. INTEREST RATES

If IP is the new *oil* of the economy, the best thing society could do would be to create liquidity in the commodity of IP. When oil was initially discovered, its status was a locked-up sludge that existed well below the earth's surface. It required expensive up-front capital and ingenuity to extract, process, manufacture into gasoline (petrol), and distribute before it created the value it provides.

Patents have a similar up-front cost to develop and find, but they lack the same liquid value-creating steps that oil has as a commodity. Absent financial liquidity, the value and price of oil would change significantly. However, since the oil market has found a process for monetization and liquidity, oil is one of the most valuable commodities in the world.

Oil's transformation from a stuck-in-the-ground commodity to a $4.3 trillion industry took decades to build. Having built the infrastructure, society will continue to extract oil from ground wells and convert it into revenues and earnings. Similarly, IP assets are a specialized commodity that requires a marketplace to break the stasis IP is currently throttled under. IP should be free flowing, and easily licensable. However, legislation and judicial outcomes have made IP monetization extremely difficult, tilting the playing field in favor of Big Tech and large companies. With the flow of IP consolidating to the largest companies in the world, and absent a free-flowing marketplace for buying, selling, and licensing IP, operating margins accrue to big companies, leaving individual and small Inventors on the outside looking in. Like oil, turning IP into the economic lifeblood of capitalism requires the extraction of IP, which currently sits frozen on the balance sheets of large companies. The balance sheet cash is fed from the river of earnings that are enriched by serial infringement.

Creating an IP marketplace is building digital infrastructure. Fortunately, the technology exists to create tools for a better flow and allocation of IP capital through our systems, but only if we have a willingness to build it. Thawing the frozen IP values subsumed by the largest companies in our society will require financial ingenuity to create transactable IP investment securities that are traded in the secondary markets of the global financial system. Without building a secondary market for IP securities, regulators will be left to fight difficult antitrust lawsuits that drag on for years and never truly address the root problems. As we saw with Microsoft during the 1990s and 2000s antitrust cases, a company like that will repurpose itself and pivot into a larger entity that is diversified yet still has oligopoly types of power.

LIAR'S POKER FOR PATENTS

In his first book, *Liar's Poker*, Michael Lewis takes us on a journey through the global bond markets in the 1980s, which Salomon Brothers investment bank dominated. The book starts by telling us of Lewis's own career out of university on Wall Street as a bond salesman in the 1980s.

A particular section of *Liar's Poker* that is instructive as an analogy to patents and IP is the idea of "information asymmetry" versus "overt market disclosures" to assist with transactional debt securities. The bond market in the 1980s operated in an opaque market with limited pricing discovery. This made transacting bonds slow and often left one side of the transaction feeling taken, which was frequently true. However, the Bloomberg Terminal created new forms of pricing discovery for buyers and sellers of bonds, resulting in a narrowing of the bid-ask prices for bonds. With bid-ask spreads narrowing, Salomon Brothers's transaction volumes increased, resulting in more profit margins, even if they were thinner on a per-transaction basis.

The transition from information asymmetry with low-volume debt transactions to liquid debt instruments with meaningful pricing discovery transformed the debt markets. Since then, the debt markets have grown to trillions in assets under management (AUM), which is several orders of magnitude larger than the equity markets.

Think about this for a moment: The total market size of all outstanding equity is $109 trillion, compared to $3.25 trillion for cryptocurrency and $315 trillion for outstanding debt. This debt comes from corporations, countries, mortgages, bank loans, and on and on. The factor that makes the entire system work is the consistency of interest payments. Investors need interest payments as part of the broader economic cycle of money.

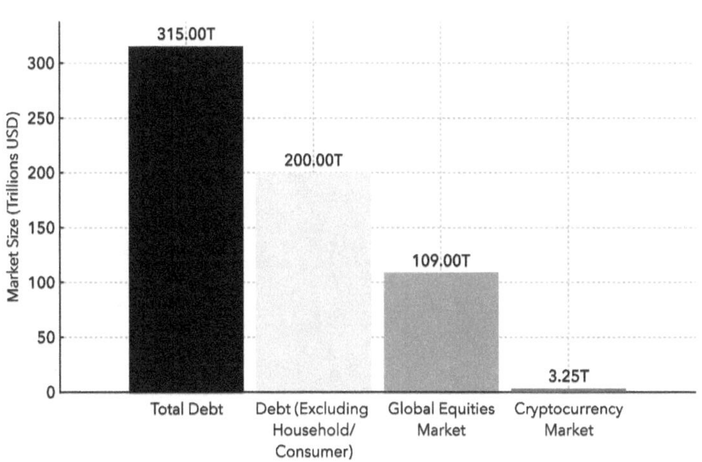

Figure 13: Global Market Sizes of Transactable Platforms

When a company takes out debt from the public markets, the investment security carries universal terms widely recognized by sophisticated investors to value and price the debt instrument. Key terms include:

- Interest rate
- Amount borrowed
- Maturity
- Coupon
- Yield to maturity

The interest rate paid is the cost of capital that creates the financial return to investors. When a company borrows money, the interest rate is paid back based on the amount borrowed until a certain return is reached for the investor. Similarly, a royalty rate can be the rate paid back for borrowed debt, until the amount is paid back in full, plus a certain return is achieved for the investor.

Figure 14: An illustrative example of the two-sided coin of interest rates and royalty rates.

Accordingly, the structure of an IP-backed debt instrument would include:

- Royalty rate on product/revenue
- Borrowed amount of debt
- Estimated maturity
- Coupon from royalty income
- "Estimated" yield to maturity

Here, the biggest difference is that the royalty fee paid to the investor is based on the level of the royalty base, rather than the amount of debt borrowed. A royalty base could be revenue, units, subscribers, or whatever the IP debt issuers decide. It is the choices and control of the IP debt issuer under the advisement of an IP investment financial professional. If the debt issuer is the Inventor *and* the commercializing entity, it creates an important combination that will create a new form of capital from an IP asset owned.

In a situation like this, how would an IP debt issuer decide what the appropriate royalty rate should be?

This is where better technical accounting for IP and Developed Technology becomes vitally important. The current financial markets work because auditors review the financial data related to a public (or private) company. Auditors provide trust and faith that the financial books are accounted for with consistency and similarity to all other public companies. Financial auditing standards, however, have flaws—big, huge, fundamental flaws when it comes to accounting for IP assets.

Examples of missing or distorted technical accounting of IP assets include:

1. lack of accounting for internally generated IP assets;
2. limited to no disclosure of third-party licensing agreements, resulting in a skewed understanding of royalty pricing;
3. tax transfer pricing and financial reporting of intangible asset valuations resulting in misstated IP values for IP assets;
4. third-party patent and IP values that have been depressed by the effort to curb patent trolls; and
5. unrecognized IP liability for unauthorized use of third-party IP.

Because intangible assets' values are siloed into unique fields and purposes when accounting for legally protected IP assets, the GAAP accounting standards for IP create a fundamental disconnect, resulting in a broad misunderstanding of value versus price for IP assets. These differences cannot be reconciled quickly or easily. Moreover, the bid-ask spread between patent holders and Implementers has never been wider or more divisive. Without a clear path toward valuing IP assets collectively, the best solution is to move IP financing to earlier in the invention and business-building process.

DISRUPTION OF FINANCIAL SECURITIES AT THE SEED OR SERIES A FUNDING LEVELS

In early-stage investing, between the seed round of financing and the Series A, an inventive startup typically moves through various stages of development and investment. The most critical step to overcome is revenue. A seed-stage startup becomes Series A eligible when revenue becomes recurring. Valuations from seed to Series A skyrocket once revenue becomes recurring! It makes an idea become investable to those with deeper pockets who are a little more risk averse.

For the founder and Inventor, his company has gone through several other gates before revenue, including: proof of concept (PoC), minimum viable product (MVP), manufacturing, distribution, marketing, launch, and, finally, scaled production. All those gates are as challenging and difficult as building annualized recurring revenue (ARR).

The time from PoC to scaled production is often called the "Startup Death Valley." It is universally accepted as one of the riskiest times in a startup's life. Being a seed stage company means only friends, family, or angel investors are willing to invest, knowing they may lose it all. Deciding where to allocate capital is hard for a founder, and legal IP protection often weighs heavy on the minds of inventive founders. In an age when Big Tech regularly steamrolls into new markets, IP protection is critical, but it often is overlooked in favor of building a viable business.

With IP becoming a secondary issue, founders focus on the stages of development toward revenue. Or they focus on fundraising, because it is hard for some inventive founders to achieve revenue without investment first. Balancing growth versus the constraints of capital, while also inventing technology that will be adopted, could be the hardest part of being an inventive founder.

IP capital solves that by underwriting future royalty income for attributed Developed Technology. This simple form of capital is already being used in several forms, such as Marvel Comic's foray into movies in the early 2000s. Or David Bowie's use of copyrights to pay for bonds the institutional markets purchased. Patented technology can take a similar form as an investment mechanism, but it requires more clarity, certainty, and predictability from the government that authorizes and enables IP protection.

While there are attempts around the world at creating an IP marketplace, the success rate is very low. An active IP marketplace in the US, for example, has been completely unsuccessful despite multiple different attempts by private enterprises. Despite trying to build an IP financing marketplace, it has proven to be too difficult. To overcome this, the US government needs infrastructure investment in the patent system to make it digital so it can leapfrog the current embattled analog system.

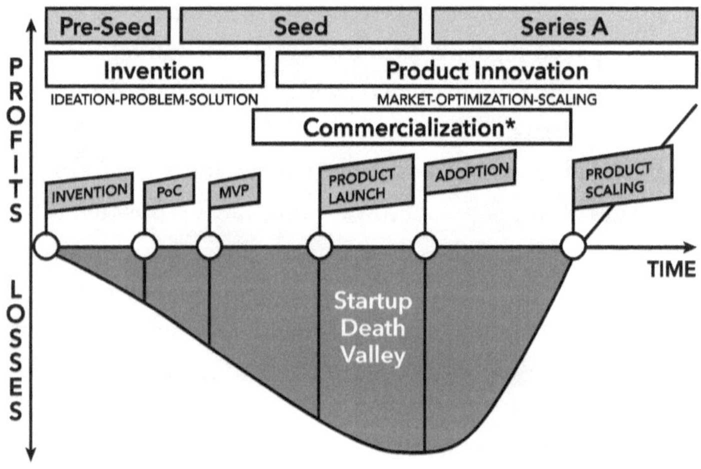

Figure 15: Startup Death Valley Life Cycle

Entrepreneurs in the "Startup Death Valley" are more willing to try new forms of finance capital, which is where IP debt capital could play a vital role. The early stage of an innovative company involves significant time and effort in product and technology development, which is often closely monitored and accounted for by the founders and investors. By building critical intangible assets and the internal tracking mechanism of their use, a foundation of IP value can be stored and accounted for, creating trust and verification for IP debt capital. Once the IP is built into a financial security explicitly tied to the founder's product, IP capital can gain traction as a meaningful financing opportunity. More aptly, if an early-stage Implementer is willing to create an FTO study with EoUs, a supportable allocation of profit margin based on the startup's selected royalty rate becomes possible.

By establishing the EoU early in the product's launch, the royalty base becomes clear. Further, the corresponding royalty rate associated with the Developed Technology becomes a cash flow stream that can be securitized for investment today with returns from future royalties tomorrow. In this regard, an investment security is created that is directly tied to the efforts, choices, and decisions of the Inventor and implementing company.

Directly connecting the IP to the product sold serves as another important factor for the IP: securing the novelty of patented invention in a commercialized product. With the royalty rate established for its product and service, an income stream can become a financialized security where the royalty rate set by the company acts like an interest rate for a company's debt, but instead it is a royalty payment attributed to the IP.

Financing Capital to IP Capital Equivalence

Equity or Debt Capital	*Equivalent to*	IP Capital as IP Equity or IP Debt
Interest Rate or Total Treasury Shares	*Equivalent to*	Royalty Rate(s) for Developed Technology and its underlying components, including Patents
Total Shares Outstanding	*Equivalent to*	IP Licensing Dividends or Royalties Paid

Figure 16: Capital investment evolves into IP Capital

Declaring a total royalty rate for Developed Technology utilized in a product or service is equivalent to an equity issuer declaring the total number of treasury shares available to be sold. Of course, very rarely do companies issue all the treasury shares. Instead, they issue a small portion; the total outstanding shares are traded in the public markets.

A company that declares a Developed Technology royalty rate creates an important precedent, particularly if the patent technology is foundational. If the technology proves likely to be used by third parties, a new stream of licensing income could be gained. It also protects investors from downside risk by making the IP assets more marketable.

With a cash flow stream directly tied to the IP, financial options become plausible because royalty income can be paid at regular intervals. Financial securities that have standardized payments on a quarterly or semiannual basis become financial instruments that can be traded on the secondary market for institutional investors.

One defining feature of financial securities backed by IP and paid for by royalties is the non-dilutive impact on equity ownership. By leveraging a company's internally generated IP to create a royalty cash flow stream, new capital strategies can be deployed for the benefit of the earliest-stage investors that financed the development of the IP in the first place. Additionally, CFOs can leverage IP without having to raise capital from new investors in a Series B or C. IP capital that follows these repayment terms can shift how capital is raised, deployed, and repaid.

For example, let us say an inventive startup is ready to raise its Series B capital round, and has already begun to receive steady revenue growth after its Series A. The company is looking to raise $25 million in its next round, which should result in high double-digit revenue growth for the next five to seven years. To raise that level of funding, the company will need an enterprise value in the $125 million to $300 million range to keep the dilutive impact of the capital raises to a minimum.

However, suppose the company has meaningfully inventive technology. In that case, it can raise IP-backed debt that can be paid back through a portion of a company's royalty income that is saved because the company invented it. Therefore, licensing payments that could have gone to a third party, but for the fact that the company owns the IP, can now be reallocated to pay back the IP debt. In this type of investment security, the IP-backed debt is repaid from cash flows from the business, and the existing shareholders are not diluted.

Additional features of IP-backed securities include:

- public disclosure of technology development rights at a high level,
- financial flexibility with opportunity to sublicense technology and IP rights to third parties,
- downside investment protection that becomes much harder to invalidate due to Inventor commercialization,
- reduced and confined financial exposure to third-party IP through the declaration of a technology rate for the product and service, and
- freedom to operate through ensuring that adopted technology is not infringing a third party's IP rights.

Some IP professionals may be surprised or they might object to an Implementer declaring a Developed Technology royalty rate at such an early stage in a company's maturation. However, if the company is acquired through M&A, the declaration of a royalty rate becomes necessary and (sometimes) compulsory through SOX (or IFRS). In fact, declaring a technology royalty rate for acquired companies occurs regularly in the context of M&A post-integration. As discussed in Chapter 3, the SOX accounting process of M&A reporting requires the valuation of Developed Technology intangibles, and the acquiring company CFO must sign off on those valuations.

The willingness of acquired companies to declare the company's royalty rate for Developed Technology is a consequential accounting measure that should be harvested as data points for IP finance securities. One of the meaningful unintended consequences of the creation of SOX-related M&A accounting has been purchase price accounting, resulting in tens of thousands of acquired companies putting a royalty rate on their own Developed Technology IP. This stated royalty rate determination can be used as a benchmark for informing a company of a reasonable royalty rate on products, which is then utilized to pay returns on IP capital securities. In this way, an IP capital issuing company has greater control on its costs, and has unique financing flexibilities. Enabling IP capital as a financial instrument is the evolution of the system that will restore balance to the economic system.

CHAPTER 5

TIMING IS EVERYTHING

"There is, in the perfect invention for the perfect moment, in the perfect context, there is real beauty. It is actual beauty, and it feels good. It's emotional. It's emotional for the inventor. It's emotional for the team that builds it. It is emotional for the customer. It is a big deal and you can feel those things."

—JEFF BEZOS, FOUNDER OF AMAZON ON THE
LEX FRIDMAN PODCAST, DECEMBER 2023

FROM BAD TO WORSE FOR RAY YARRIS

Ray and his FIL realized they would need to pivot their business again in 2016. What had started as an exciting entrepreneurial family business had taken a turn. Ray and his wife were constantly fighting. The anticipation of losing the biggest and only client they had was causing a rift. Moreover, Ray and his FIL were not getting along, and the decision to employ Ray's brother-in-law (BIL) as a salesperson only worsened the tension.

"I don't want to become a patent troll," Ray told me in one of our initial conversations about the patent valuation he hired me to complete in late 2016. While there were numerous strategic options for Ray to consider, turning his patent into a litigation program was a monetization decision of last resort.

A lot had changed in the three years since he had last hired me to value his patents. When I first completed the patent valuation in 2013, Part 2 of the AIA had just been enacted. The legislature had suggested that the PTAB would limit litigation and enable licensing, but by 2016, it was clear: The AIA's PTAB was a bludgeoning hammer that invalidated almost any patent that came before it.

Most of what was presented to the PTAB involved parallel patent infringement litigation. It creates a dual-track process for patent litigation that conflicts with itself, causing extreme harm to patent holders. In an IP subcommittee hearing in early January 2024, one of the original authors of the AIA testified under oath that the law "is not being used as it was intended."

One of Ray's primary goals was not to lose his patent to the IPR, and we could feel the pressure of the AIA's outcomes weighing on our strategic options. If he wanted to truly know the value of his patents, he would need to be certain his patents were being used by the slew of third parties identified, if he had to go to litigation. So, we hired technical subject matter experts in "software storage capacity and transfer" to conduct an infringement analysis. The technical expert was able to create multiple "Rule 11" grade EoU claim charts using multiple patent claims from Ray's patents. And it was created for multiple companies, over and over. Ray's patent claims had become an almost textbook-like document, training cloud companies on how to best optimize network capacity for backing up data. The patent was foundational for cloud service providers, and most could not help but infringe on the patents.

After having the technical expert build six different Rule 11

EoUs, and one litigation-ready EoU, we circled back together to discuss our next options. There was still one deal-killer issue to work through, and it was a bit like eating Japanese blowfish sushi: Do it right and everything will be fine (or perhaps amazing), but do it wrong and the patent is killed. The killer issues were twofold: prior art and the Alice Corporation ruling from the Supreme Court of the United States (SCOTUS).

For Ray's patent, the initial efforts for finding prior art by patent examiners at the time of the patent application was a defective process. Many sophisticated patent professionals believed that many prior art references had been missed during the initial examination process. The PTAB and IPR processes allow for prior art to be reconsidered, and almost all patent litigations involve a renewed effort to invalidate the patent using prior art that was not previously reviewed.

So, it begged the question: Should Ray conduct a prior art search to see if there were invalidating references in the public domain? If we got the right feedback on prior art, the threat of invalidation would be reduced, but not eliminated. However, if we found invalidating prior art, the risk of losing the patent increased significantly.

The next gating factor for Ray is the software enabling his patent, which became challenged after a SCOTUS ruling called "Alice" that severely limited software patents' likelihood. Since it was a legal question, the attorneys we spoke with believed there was a strong likelihood of surviving an IPR, but it was impossible to know. It was a risky proposition to attempt enforcement. Trying patent litigation would certainly lead to an IPR, and then what? If an IPR invalidated the patent, it would vanish.

Ray and his family could not stand to have the patent vanish. An incredible amount of time, investment, and business had been built on the expectation that the patent would provide meaningful benefits for being the first Inventor of a broadly used technology. However, behind the scenes of valuing his patent, his business was breaking apart, and his family would become estranged. The only glue that held the family business together were the patents Ray had invented, and the hopes that there could be restitution from the industry for using his patent without authorization.

Ray was under exceptional pressure. He wanted to have a clean divorce and to break away from his ex-wife and in-laws after an exceptionally hard decade as an entrepreneur. The finger-pointing between Ray and his in-laws for not securing a renewed service agreement with their only client was palpable. The only thing holding these people together was the company's potential sale or monetization of its patent portfolio. Until then, they were stuck together.

When we finally completed the valuation of Ray's patents in 2016, it was clear that he had a high-value patent that was foundational to the industry. The question was whether buyers would be interested in acquiring his company at the price he wanted. Ray was not interested in a patent licensing and litigation campaign, despite the broad-sweeping infringement by numerous entities. Based on historical and forecast revenues of the infringers, the damages calculations for infringement ranged from $5 million to $75 million respectively, with a total aggregated value close to $150 million across the identified group of infringers.

For an outright sale of the patents, however, the price was closer to $750,000 to $2,000,000, much lower than what Ray and his company would want to sell the patents for. The range of outcomes, depending on the monetization method, was disconcerting. If the patent litigations won, Ray and his family stood to earn tens of millions of dollars. If they lost, the potential outcome would be a complete loss of the patents and income. Therefore, it was discombobulating news to provide a wide range of value outcomes for the patents, at a time of great personal upheaval for Ray and his family.

INVENTION IS ICONIC

Ingenuity and invention are represented by the light bulb turning on in the brain. Thomas Edison is an iconic Inventor who created the light bulb, which eventually turned into General Electric (GE), one of the most important companies in the US in the twentieth century. The light bulb was an invented discovery that made life better and more efficient. As a result, humans recognized that anyone can have the "light bulb of creative invention" go on in the mind, yet only a small portion of society will take the invention and turn it into a patent.

Applying for a patent is a meaningful task that carries extraordinary risk. The application process is difficult and requires professional assistance to liaise with the US Patent Office. The US Patent Office is the gatekeeper and decision-maker. They seek to ensure another person has not invented the same idea first. This is why timing is so important when filing for a patent. Even if the idea or concepts you have for your invention came years before you applied for a patent, if another Inventor files for a similar patent prior to you, the other Inventor will receive the patent because they filed first. The technology you may have been using for years is now someone else's unless you documented the invention first and can invalidate their patent through prior art.

"First to file" was one of the defining features of the AIA. It replaced the previous "first to invent" process, bringing the US in line with the rest of the world's patent offices, but hindsight suggests that this change has given a unique advantage to large companies over individuals or smaller companies, who patent less frequently. While this feature of the AIA was lauded and praised, the outcome has led to unintended consequences, primarily leading to lower patenting levels for individuals and small companies.

The process and timing of obtaining a patent are troubling under the AIA's change. In an ideal world, an Inventor would have the light bulb of invention go on, apply for a patent, and the issuance of granted patents would help create a commercialization lane of opportunity for the patent owner. It would appear like this:

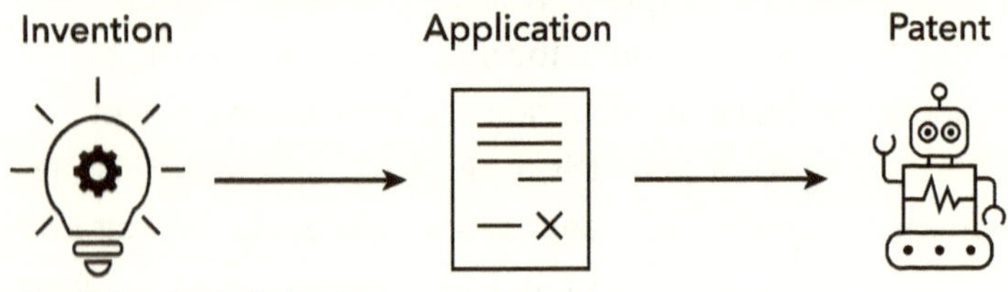

Figure 17: Invention, Application, Patent

The simple three-step path that most individual Inventors expect is quite different than the illustration. In reality, the granting of a patent requires passing a series of binary gate thresholds, some of which are well known, but many that are unknown due to the AIA's legislative changes. Due to the gating thresholds, a granted US patent holds limited value due to the PTAB, a post-grant proceeding that introduces the risk of future invalidation, thereby undermining its worth. Accordingly, the window of opportunity for a patent to become commercialized by the Inventor himself is shorter than it has ever been for small and individual Inventors.

Larger entities can try to move quickly against startups, but they have also learned that going slowly and replicating or simulating similar technology in the marketplace at lower price points as a second mover is highly advantageous. When larger companies begin infringing on a smaller company's patents, pursuing legal recourse for the patent holder becomes a burden. Patent enforcement is expensive, time-consuming, mentally taxing, and carries the extraordinary risk of losing the patent and accompanying investment alongside the patent.

Moreover, the last decade has put Inventors without a business model for their invention at great risk. As part of the sea change that has occurred in the previous fifteen years, patented Inventors who do not attempt to commercialize their own invention into businesses, but have the audacity to enforce their IP rights, are much more susceptible to being invalidated if they try to enforce their patent rights.

Part of the overarching narrative that has been widely accepted is that Inventors who do not become entrepreneurs will eventually become patent trolls, an unfair and incredibly hard characterization to overcome when enforcing patent rights. Most horrifically, for many small Inventors, seeking to enforce patent rights can be the harshest way to lose the patented rights via the IPR process, giving away for free what previously had been protected.

During the process of application, prosecution, and grant, the proposed patent goes through a never-ending series of binary gates. If the patent fails the test presented at the binary gate, the patent is lost. When passing through the gates, it is usually a coin-flip type of decision determining whether or not the patent will continue its journey, or it may be completely dismantled, rendering it useless to its Inventor. A few examples of the gated thresholds include the following:

- Novel and nonobvious
- Prior art searching: validity versus invalidity
- Freedom to operate versus evidence of use

These factors directly impact a licensing fee estimate for using patented technology. Each factor has a direct impact on estimating the valuation and pricing of patent assets. Creating uncertainty in those factors is a purpose-built roadblock to undermine patent value.

THE LARGEST BILLION-DOLLAR PATENT PORTFOLIO

Nortel Networks (Nortel) was the largest Chapter 7 bankruptcy liquidation in Canadian history, creating over $2 billion in professional fees for the advisors overseeing the liquidation sale of the company's assets. With over $33 billion in debt, the recovery of lost investment required the sale of a handful of profitable businesses and the company's 3,600 global patents. Most analysts believed the Nortel patents would be sold for nine figures, but the stalking-horse bid process created a flurry of activity between two consortiums of buyers, led by Apple on one side and Google on the other.

Nortel's patents held extraordinary value to the smartphone industry. Unencumbered by licenses to third parties, numerous standard essential patents (SEPs), or fundamental patents necessary for the rise in smartphones, the auction sale of the patents was an absolute blockbuster. Add in all the patent trolls vying for an opportunity to monetize the patents, and a frothy bidding process during the auction led to a $4.5 billion price tag, the highest amount ever paid for a patent portfolio and one that may never be seen again. The final price was fourteen times higher than the initial stalking-horse bid of $314,285,714.28 by Google (in a nod to π).

The unexpected windfall from the patent sale in the liquidation process created a fight among Nortel's global creditors, and my employer at the time, Ocean Tomo, was hired to help support the European debtors in the allocation of proceeds. Nearly $8 billion in capital had been recovered during the liquidation process, and now it had to be allocated to three primary groups: (1) the US private equity investors, (2) the Canadian pensioners, and (3) the European debt investors (who represented creditors from the rest of the world, too). The battle over allocating capital to the three groups was bruising, intense, and always had a short timeline.

Simultaneously, Cengage, a college textbook publisher acquired by a group of private equity (PE) firms several years earlier, had encountered financial difficulties in repaying the nearly $7 billion in debt that the PEs had invested in the publisher. The publisher's operations were doing fairly well but not good enough to pay the exorbitant interest expenses that came with the debt. The debt needed to be restructured, and a similar fight between the various creditors loomed. Ocean Tomo was again hired to help the publisher value the company's copyrights, which would help restructure the debt to manageable levels. Again, the battle was bruising, intense, and always had a short timeline.

Never before and never again in my career will two projects of such gigantic size and scope run parallel paths like Nortel and Cengage.

After nearly a year of intense effort, the reallocation of investment value for both companies, theoretically based on the value of IP assets, had become a fool's errand. Negotiated settlement amounts were determined not because of the IP values, but because lawyers and judges in the proceedings found other ways to divide the remaining assets of two bankrupt companies.

The mystery of IP valuation was unsolved in both cases.

It is the inability to accurately assess the value and price of a patent portfolio that has caused the system and its participants so much pain and suffering. This dichotomy between value and price has undermined countless inventor's patents, and Ray's patents were deeply harmed because of the AIA.

THE LONG JOURNEY CONTINUES FOR RAY YARRIS'S STRATEGIC MONETIZATION

The risk of invalidation is unusually high for patent Inventors who were awarded patents between 1999 and 2011, especially for software patents. A series of precedential SCOTUS outcomes, including Alice, plus the AIA law change during the midterm of a patent's life, will do that. For Ray Yarris, the changes from the AIA plus Alice completely undermined his patent portfolio, but the extent of the damages was not known until he tried to enforce his patents for unauthorized use.

It was late 2016, and I was working with Houlihan Lokey. Only three years into the AIA's PTAB provision, there was still a general hope that individual Inventors might be able to sell or license its portfolio, or at least that is what I had come to believe. Houlihan Lokey, however, had different ideas. The opportunity to help Ray at Houlihan Lokey was considered too small and risky. Moreover, several other small company Inventors had inquired about IP valuations, and they too were too small of opportunities, so I decided to take those clients and strike out on my own.

With a handful of clients coming with me, including Ray Yarris, my focus was helping individuals, small companies, or early-stage entrepreneurs secure financing for growth or IP defense/monetization. The technical advisor I partnered with to build EoUs from Ray Yarris's patents was finding potential infringement by several cloud companies. The developed claim charts were created to help sell the business along with the software, the API, and the SDK, which Ray had written himself. We knew that potential operating company buyers might downplay the patents' importance, so we marketed the patents as an "add-on" to acquiring the software IP.

From there, I ran an auction sale process. I started outreach on behalf of Self-Server to potential buyers in February 2017. There were over forty companies on the initial list of potential buyers. If the operating companies expressed no interest in buying, I had plan B, plan C, and even plan D to help find interested investors.

After reaching out to about twenty companies, a short list of interested buyers emerged. Conversations with a variety of in-house IP teams took place, and a couple of potential buyers signed NDAs to receive the longer form investment deck, and to enter the data room. By April, two potential buyers were completing due diligence, and one of the interested buyers asked for a software demonstration.

The potential buyer's main technical team was located in California, so the Self-Server team and I headed to their location for an in-person meeting. We rented a meeting space in the WeWork near the company's headquarters, and got together for a discussion. Ray was the main star of the discussion. He and the potential buyer's technical team spent nearly an hour talking through the software, how it operated, and the benefits his software had over alternatives.

As the conversation went on, the technical expert was getting increasingly animated with incredible interest in the software's capabilities. The buyer's technical expert was well versed in the technology, and understood the importance of Ray's software as he reviewed the documents before him.

"We do something verrry similar to what you're describing, but it requires a lot of network capacity," the technical advisor said.

"Well, the Self-Server software will reduce the network capacity by hashing data using identifiers so that the same data that already exists at the other location won't be sent over the network," Ray said.

"Ooh, I see how you are doing this now. I get it. Is this what your software does? Is this also in your patent?"

"Yes, it is what the software does, and it is part of the patent claims," Ray responded.

"Oh my! I guess we should get a license for the patent even if we do not make a deal," the buyer's technical expert suggested.

The conversation went on for some time, and when it came time for a demonstration, Ray opened his computer and loaded the software onto his screen that was shared on the big monitor. He went through the demonstration, but it was not the same demonstration he had previously shown me. It was shorter, and less impactful. The technician was not impressed by the end, and I was gobsmacked. I could not believe that the demo had gone so poorly. Everything was going great until Ray opened his computer.

The meeting ended with overtures to continue discussions. Ray knew he had underwhelmed the buyer's technical advisor and promised to show a better demonstration the next time they spoke. Unfortunately, Ray never got another opportunity to show his demonstration again. He had one shot to get it right and he blew it.

The buyer's C-suite lost interest in the software, and ended up passing on the purchase. A few months after the meeting, I called the CFO of the potential buyer and I let him know that they should make an offer to buy Self-Server. And if they did not want to buy, they should make an offer to license the patents and IP. I reminded the CFO what the technical advisor had said about taking a license, but he politely declined to take a license or make an offer to purchase.

The remaining operating company buyers all started to move away from the opportunity. The interest in buying a defensive patent asset did not elicit a strong response from operating companies. It was time to shift to Plan B and C: patent monetization and patent litigation firms.

In the second phase of outreach to buyers, several enforcement agent investors emerged. After talking to several groups, a mid-tier Washington, DC–based patent litigation attorney became interested in litigating the patent portfolio. He had concerns about a potential IPR if they entered broad-sweeping litigation against all potential infringers as a collective. Accordingly, he recommended a slow-and-steady plan of sequential and serial litigations. The litigator suggested this as a means to halt collective IPR action from a group, and instead force each alleged infringer to decide if they wanted to IPR the patents alone.

The sequential and serial litigation plan would be a slow process, but it was the most viable monetization option Self-Server could obtain from litigation attorneys or funders. Self-Server signed a fully contingent patent litigation agreement with the new patent litigating attorney, who got to work building a litigation case.

While Ray was uncomfortable with the plan to monetize via patent litigation, there were no other options, given that we had tried all the friendly monetization options earlier. Now was the time to use the stick of enforcement. With the five-year contractual operating agreement with their client coming to an end, and no operating companies interested in buying the company, patent litigation seemed to be the only path forward for Self-Server. It was at this point that my official capacity ended with Self-Server. The litigation attorney took over from there.

First up for litigation was the company that sent a technical advisor to meet with Self-Server in person. The DC litigator filed a patent complaint against the company by the end of 2017. A few days later, my phone rang.

"WHAT THE HELL ARE YOU DOING?!" a screaming voice yelled at me as I answered the phone.

"I'm sorry, who is this?"

"It is Jim Bouche [of the potential buying company]. You purposefully planned to set us up for patent litigation! You're a crook!" he screamed at me.

"I'm sorry, but these guys have strong IP and your technical expert suggested that you should take a license. I explicitly asked you to take one several months ago and you declined. What did you expect would happen?" I responded.

"Not this! This is bullshit and you know it."

"I disagree, and I strongly recommend you work to settle this out. I am no longer involved with this process. I tried to sell the patents. Now someone else is leading the litigation."

"Yeah, right," he said. "You're a sonvabitch!"

"Okay, nice talking to you," I said, and we hung up.

SATOSHI NODA AND PATENT STRATEGIES

CHAPTER 6

DISRUPTING CREDIT CARDS

*"Picasso had a saying: 'Good artists copy, great artists steal.' And you know, we have always been **shameless** about stealing great ideas."*

—STEVE JOBS, FOUNDER OF APPLE (EMPHASIS HIS)

Apple Pay was first introduced in 2014, during the iPhone 6 release presentation. However, the process of developing Apple Pay had started long before, with Apple investing in R&D, seeking acquisitions of fintech startups (e.g., acquiring competitor employees through acqui-hires), and securing patents before launching. In its earliest iterations, before Apple Pay was released, the critical component Apple was seeking to replace was the magnetic stripe credit card that was swiped at the point-of-sale at merchant retail stores. The credit card industry first used the magnetic stripe in the 1980s, but it was proven to be susceptible to theft, and it was ready to be disrupted by new technology. Apple realized this but did not know which form factor would replace the magnetic stripe.

Starbucks had been working on its own smartphone payment app, and rumors swirled that a quick response (QR) code was the planned method for replacing the swipe. Separately, Target made headlines in 2013 after being hacked using the old-fashioned magnetic stripe that allowed for mirroring of credit card information that could be used in another location. The threat to credit cards being displaced by smartphones was real, and contactless payment technology offered more security and had better access controls. However, the debate over the form factor for contactless payments was anyone's guess in the late aughts and early 2010s.

Apple researched various contactless payment options using a smartphone in 2006, including QR codes, near-field communications (NFC), radio frequency identification (RFID), and/or Bluetooth. Each of those wireless communication methods has its own unique properties with benefits and detractions for implementation in an electronic payment process. In 2007, Apple reached out to Inventor Satoshi Noda (not his real name) to request his expert assistance, and he began attending meetings with a new standard-setting organization for an electronic payment system through devices. The group included Apple, Microsoft, and Google.

Satoshi is a prolific Inventor who moved to California from Japan when he was sixteen to attend California Polytechnic State University (Cal Poly). After finishing his undergrad by nineteen, he was accepted to Stanford, receiving a double PhD in electrical engineering and computer science. Shortly after, he began working for Denso Wave, a subsidiary of the Japanese automotive parts company. Denso Wave is known for having the largest barcode patent registry in the world, largely due to Satoshi's work. While at Denso from 1998 until 2003, Satoshi was named Inventor on over 110 granted patents assigned to Denso.

Satoshi is like most Inventors: introverted and understated.

Standing at six feet tall with thinning black hair and glasses, Satoshi carries himself like a professor despite being the CEO of three different startups and sitting on the board of directors for another six companies. Satoshi's technical prowess is unmatched, and his various engineering teams laud his working style. Satoshi is keenly aware of issues related to the technical problems before they arise and often helps his teams troubleshoot issues in real time. For this reason, his teams are highly dedicated to him, and he is sought out as a leader in his field.

In 2004, Satoshi left Denso to launch his own company in fintech (short for financial technology), and he started it out of his house in Mountain View, California. He was living his American dream. By 2006, he was in contact with several companies, including Apple, Stripe, Venmo, Starbucks, Walmart, Microsoft, and Google. Satoshi continued to invent at a steady pace and by 2014, when Apple Pay was introduced, Satoshi's startup company had an additional seventy-five patents issued with Satoshi as the named Inventor.

Satoshi had heard many people tell him to be wary of going to Apple for any meeting because they had a reputation for feigning interest in a startup company's products. Apple would then project a willingness to invest in the startup, but it would lead to a ghosting by the Apple acquisition team, and eventually the startup's technology, trade secrets, and patents would end up in Apple's product without authorization. Examples of this type of problem are everywhere.

When Apple finally called Satoshi, he joined them for a few high-level meetings but never went under a nondisclosure agreement (NDA) and never shared any of his trade secret information, despite Apple's team poking and prodding for specific details about sensor hardware compatibility and encryption techniques.

"Apple was fishing for information when I met with them. It did not feel right to engage with them, so I backed away politely. They clearly figured out what I was on to, and they came to the exact invention to mine on their own," Satoshi recollected of his meetings with Apple.

Eventually, Satoshi pivoted his entire business into a new segment of financial services, in large part because of the challenge of competing with Big Tech in the device payments space. It was obvious that his inventions would be taken without authorization if he continued working with the newly created "electronic payment" standard-setting organization, so he pivoted like any smart and savvy entrepreneur. His new startup was focused on providing back-office support for the information technology (IT) of professional investment managers and their clients (e.g., Fidelity, Oppenheimer, Empower, etc.). The unique niche has provided him access to a wide range of banking and financial relationship connections, and his inventions have led to two other startups, and the conceptual plan for several other companies.

I met Satoshi in the summer of 2019, and his board of directors had tasked him to monetize his most valuable patent assets. He explained the background of his inventions to me, and I got a team of technical experts mining his portfolio of patents to understand and uncover where the value was hidden. After portfolio-mining his patents, we found six exceptional patent families foundational to contactless smartphone payment technology. The patents covered multiple aspects of payment from a device, and we conducted a high-level estimate of damages. The litigation damages estimates were in the low billions on the most conservative of estimates, and it did not include the new payment method related to wearable devices like the Apple Watch.

Satoshi's team and I conferred at the end of a six-week analysis, taking stock of the critical evidence of use (EoU) charts that read on every device that enables mobile contactless payments. Phones plus smartwatches make for a gigantic royalty base of infringing products, so the effort to invalidate Satoshi's patents will come from all sides once the litigation starts.

"Have you considered attempting to negotiate a friendly license with the infringers rather than initiating a litigation out of the gate?" I asked Satoshi in our strategy meeting.

"Not after my meetings with them a few years back. It became very clear to me a long time ago that they would resist any attempts to ask for a license at a reasonable price," Satoshi replied.

We knew that friendly patent licenses occurred occasionally, but smartphone makers are more likely to engage in cross-licensing of patent portfolios with other large technology companies. They were not inclined to pay patent licensing fees to small firms. Not without a litigation fight first. For a small Inventor like Satoshi, big entities like Apple or Samsung would undoubtedly tell Satoshi to take his patents and go pound sand with them. It was a vexing situation.

After considering all the other varied patent monetization strategies for Satoshi, we decided to find patent litigation funding. Our team conducted a targeted auction process to several litigation funders and contingent litigators to aid with a patent enforcement plan. To conduct the capital raise process, we took the following steps to prepare for a litigation funder:

- finalized the patent family's EoUs,
- made marketing collateral about the IP,
- filled a data room with industry information about contactless payment systems, and
- built a top-notch financial damages model.

The outreach for patent litigation funders required that Satoshi find the right patent litigators, too. With parallel outreach efforts underway, we ultimately found litigation funders and patent litigators simultaneously. Since Satoshi's patents had such strong EoUs, the interest in funding his litigations was strong. Nearly every contact we made was interested, and we were in full swing of courting potential litigation funders in January 2020. By late February, I had four separate term sheets from interested parties to fund a patent litigation campaign.

And then COVID-19 hit.

Two of the investors pulled their term sheets. The world's financial markets were in chaos, and the steep sell-off in March 2020 led to many exceptional businesses being sold at deeply discounted prices. Investing in anything else would have been easier than investing in Satoshi's patent litigations, which had the terrifying task of taking on the most valuable companies in the world. Trying to reel in one of the litigation funders still at the table would be a herculean task as the world was shutting down.

The two remaining bidders had made starkly different terms to invest in Satoshi's patent litigation effort. The first offer was from a stalwart of the litigation funding business. The second was a family office investor looking for uncorrelated returns to the stock market. The patriarch of the family office was getting into the technical minutia of the infringement analysis and EoUs. He was a septuagenarian who enjoyed a good fight, and he was quite keen to get into it with Apple and Samsung. The family office was offering an up-front payment but a much lower back end on the result of the patent litigation. The traditional litigation funder was offering no up-front but two and a half times more on the back end. It was a classic betting man's gamble because patent litigation is a flip of the coin, so is it better to lock in a return now, with less later? Or hold out on early funds coming in, with the expectation of a bigger return later?

It was a tense couple of months analyzing and strategizing the two litigation funding offers, but Satoshi eventually received board approval to accept the traditional litigation funder's offer, and the family office was left to find another patent battle to finance. It was another six months before we could close the financing because of the depth of prior art searching conducted before the closing. It was a stressful wait to hear back on the prior art results, but there were no surprises. Now, Satoshi is waiting for the patent litigators to complete their work, which is often a five- to ten-year wait.

In the years after I helped Satoshi, the European Union (EU) announced a potential $27 billon fine on Apple for its closed NFC payment system, which Satoshi invented. Satoshi's invention is the foundational technology that enables Apple Pay and Samsung Pay. The EU's fine calculation was based on the same damages calculations supporting Satoshi's patent damages, a per-unit payment for all violating devices. That's 1.38 billion iPhones and over 100 million Apple Watches.

In 2024, the EU's pressure forced Apple to agree to allow third-party payment service providers to use Apple Pay. The tremendously large fine acted as a deterrent for continued bad actions and speaks to the potential damages Satoshi could be awarded in a patent litigation. Apple's move to be conciliatory toward EU regulators is a sign that they can be flexible, but it only comes after the harshest of penalties is suggested. Said differently, Apple requires the threat of litigation with outsized fees for them to become reasonable.

Ultimately, Apple is a patent pariah. No other US company has been accused of patent theft as frequently as Apple. Only

Samsung has more patent litigations against it, but they are a much larger company with a more extensive product offering than Apple. On a per-product basis, no one has been sued more for patent infringement than Apple. It has created extraordinary financial exposure, and Apple fights with every means possible against every assertion of IP infringement. Satoshi is one of thousands of Inventors with an axe to grind against Apple.

WINNING THE INNOVATION RACE VS. FAILURES IN INNOVATION

For every successful unicorn startup story, there is a counter-vailing example of a unicorn's total financial devastation. While Elon Musk (SpaceX, Tesla, SolarCity, X/Twitter) and Jeff Bezos (Amazon) have captured lightning in a bottle with their inventive and innovative companies, Elizabeth Holmes (Theranos), Adam Neumann (WeWork), and Sam Bankman-Fried (FTX) have proven that the "cult of personality" investment practice can be devastating to the success of a unicorn. Regardless of these failures, America's VC investment practices focus on chasing growth rather than creating exceptional technology. For VCs, high-quality technology invention and creation is inevitable, but growing that technology is not. Since patents act as a speed bump for startups, and patents are a deeply undervalued asset, its importance has been trivialized and undermined. Industries such as cloud computing, blockchain, 3D printing, quantum computing, and now artificial intelligence (AI) are among the hyped-up technology advancements that have undergone the economic cycle of outsized investment, retrenchment, reconsideration, and repricing. It happens like clockwork during every business cycle.

Lost in hype are the Inventors in the trenches, like Satoshi and Ray. Great inventive minds who rely upon the US patent system to protect them from the large incumbents whose invention processes are less than those of the Inventor working out of his home. Despite all the fantastic resources, financial support, and high-tech labs, large incumbents regularly fail to see the invention in the same way the individual Inventor sees it. When a large incumbent that has mastered innovation but not invention sees another Inventor's ideas, it will incorporate the invention as part of its R&D process.

Examples of invention "borrowing" among Big Tech abound. For example, TikTok's unique video-sharing platform allows users to create their own videos to "inspire others and create joy." The platform has created millions of content creators, and the consumers of that content absorb the information through "doomscrolling," the act of mindlessly watching videos on a phone or computer for hours at a time. TikTok consumers spent the most hours "doomscrolling" compared to all the other social media platforms. As a result, Facebook, Instagram, X/Twitter, YouTube, and even LinkedIn all created their own versions of TikTok's video sharing. Now all the social media outlets provide doomscrolling videos, a business practice initially created by TikTok.

Technology companies are in the business of "borrowing" ideas from others. It is not quite "stealing" in their minds because they are adjusting them, making changes that activate their own spin on the invention. When it happens between large incumbents, it is one thing, but when it happens to individual Inventors trying to innovate, it becomes devastating.

CHAPTER 7

INVESTOR HELL

"AOL remains deeply undervalued today despite the recent increase in stock price driven by the announced sale of a substantial majority of AOL's patent portfolio to Microsoft Corporation for $1.056 billion."

—STARBOARD VALUE INVESTMENT FUND TO AMERICA
ONLINE BOARD OF DIRECTORS, MAY 7, 2012

DISRUPTION STARTS SMALL BEFORE IT BECOMES OBVIOUS

A defining feature of Satoshi's persona is the little green leather-bound notebook he carries with him. It is his invention notebook, which he keeps in his pocket, so he is ready to scribble notes and ideas when the creative light bulb goes on. He showed me the bookshelf of his invention diaries, which had numerous rows of the exact same green leather-bound books in chronological order.

Most of the green invention books have been thoughtfully used. The spines are faded white. The pages have tags and dog-ears. Notes in English and Japanese, diagrams, mathematical equations, and illustrations fill the pages of each book. He pulls the invention book from 2006, showing his inventive process for contactless payment systems using a phone. The diagrams are a prelude to what is put into the patents he has been granted. Moreover, he shows me a video of the various stages of experimental trials he undertook with his team to determine the correct calculations, algorithms, encryption techniques, and form factors for his inventions.

Like most Inventors, most of the first attempts to solve the problem failed.

"For me, it is about mathematics and diagrams in my head. Building it for the first time becomes easier once I visualize my invention through equations and simulations. It usually becomes a bit harder as we move beyond discovery to trials or production. Still, it has always been exciting for me to experiment, adjust, and try again," Satoshi says of his invention process.

After numerous attempts and tweaks, *eureka!* Satoshi has solved the issue that was scrambling the outcome he was hoping to see. A few adjustments and notes are written in his book in red pen to highlight the enabling changes he discovered. He says these meticulous notes help prove his invention process is accurate, and it has helped him on several occasions with patent examinations.

"Invention is an iterative process. I have a goal in mind, and through the experimentation process, more inventive steps and ideas are discovered. Once an inventive process starts, it can be quite consuming," Satoshi says. "And after concentrated focus, inventions start self-generating [in my mind]. That's why I have been able to write so many patents. The invention process inevitably results in numerous ideas with patentable claims.

"The way the AIA is written now, the green invention book

is not as valuable as it once was." Satoshi is referring to the provisions of the America Invents Act, which changed the invention filing status to "first to file" rather than "first to invent." Opponents of this portion of the AIA suggest that this gives large companies that frequently file more direct early access to examiners. Proponents say it aligns the US with the rest of the world. Ultimately, it has made it harder for the individual Inventor to keep pace with Big Tech.

THE BUSINESS CYCLE WITH INTELLECTUAL PROPERTY

Conventional wisdom suggests businesses go through a four-stage cycle:

1. Expansion
2. Peak
3. Contraction
4. Trough

For each business, the cycle it goes through is highly dependent on *when* in the economic cycle the business launches. Timing business cycles and economic cycles is a nearly impossible task, and serendipity often plays a big role. Sometimes, it is more impactful than strategic planning.

For early-stage companies that cannot overcome the fourth stage (trough), the fifth stage of the cycle is *failure.* In the event of failure, what becomes of the company's assets is a question of context and circumstance. Prior to the AIA, IP assets that were foundational technology maintained recovery value that could restore lost investment in a business. For failing start-ups, creating, owning, and monetizing IP is meant to provide strategic protection against potential infringers. However, the

AIA's IPR process has upended recovery values of patent portfolios, resulting in the complete and total loss of investment in a meaningful portion of startup companies. The changes have altered how VCs, private equity, and family offices (collectively referred to as "VCs") invest into startups, and how they view IP in those situations.

PATENTING STRATEGY FOR STARTUPS

Theranos, the infamous medical device company that claimed to revolutionize blood testing, was founded by Elizabeth Holmes in 2003 when she was nineteen. Ten years later, Theranos was a Silicon Valley darling, reaching a peak valuation of $9 billion. By 2016, however, the revolutionary company was under investigation for fraudulently misleading investors and the market by falsifying outcomes from its devices. Investigations found that Ms. Holmes had been lying about what her devices could achieve. Ms. Holmes, a named Inventor on dozens of patents, ultimately landed herself in prison as a convicted felon.

At the start, however, Elizabeth was counting on the patent system to help protect her business from potential infringers. Blood testing diagnostic was ready for disruption, and Elizabeth was the revolutionary who planned to make it happen. Unfortunately, she was too early. The technology she envisioned was not ready to become a minimum viable product (MVP), and no matter how strong her will was, the technology was not ready for production.

When the deception was finally revealed, the company had moved into the trough and finally bankruptcy stage of failure. Since the underlying IP and patent strategy at Theranos had been robust, by the end of its life cycle, the company owned over seven hundred patents. Theranos and its investors placed a significant emphasis on patents to protect the company and its investments. In the waning days of its existence, Fortress Investment Group (Fortress) offered Theranos a final lifeline through an IP-backed patent portfolio investment.

Fortress came in as the "white knight" investor and provided a $100 million loan to assist the company through its trough cycle. While the investment required hitting certain operational milestones, the likelihood of hitting those marks would be nearly impossible. Ultimately, Fortress came in and swooped up Theranos's patent portfolio for a song compared to the R&D that went into it.

While Elizabeth's fate was being sealed, the ongoing journey of the Theranos patents continued on, becoming a part of the story when COVID-19 hit. Controversy over the patent portfolio became public in March 2020 when a subsidiary of Fortress litigated the use of the patents against bioMérieux SA, a French biotech firm working on COVID-19-related testing.

Patent critics and the US government excoriated Fortress for litigating patents that could be used in the treatment of the global pandemic. Fortress quickly responded by offering the patents on a royalty-free basis "to any third party working on diagnostics tests directed to COVID-19," but it did not matter. Detractors suggested that the Theranos patents had been received fraudulently through Elizabeth Holmes, even though the investor fraud had little to do with the patents themselves. In fact, the chief scientist and named Inventor on dozens of Theranos patents, Ian Gibbons, had been the true source of inventive technology at the embattled company.

Ian Gibbons's inventions were meaningful and significant, even if controversial. Gibbons was integral to realizing Holmes's vision to provide quick and simple diagnostic testing regardless of the fraudulence. Moreover, Fortress's patent investment group is a highly sophisticated operator in the patent space. They do not invest in "nuisance patents" made infamous by predatory patent trolls. Instead, they seek arbitrage in the patent system where Implementers are trying to skirt the rules by using another's patents without compensation. Sadly, Ian Gibbons became so distraught over the entire situation that he died by suicide in 2013, a situation that Gibbons's wife blames solely on his employment with Theranos.

LOST INVESTMENT RECOVERY

Sadly, the AIA has taken one of the tools of business recovery, patents, and turned it into a wasting asset with dangerous unintended consequences for the patent owner seeking to enforce its patent rights. Investment recovery through the sale or monetization of assets is a critical component of investing that is often overlooked. Companies fail for many reasons, and Theranos's failure, while unique to the story, has an ending that is fairly common: patent enforcement agents (i.e., Fortress) come seeking to monetize the patents from the failed company.

While startups fail for a myriad of reasons, IP theft is undeniably a cause of startup failure, and it happens more often than people realize. It is a parasitic problem where technology transfer occurs without compensation, resulting in a total investment loss for investors of the failed startups.

In the early 2000s, VC investors unwittingly took the story of patent trolls so seriously that they cut off their noses to spite their faces. VCs saw the problems caused by increased patent litigation in their portfolio companies, and jumped on the bandwagon for legislative change. It was easy to join the chorus of voices denouncing patent litigation. There were stories in the news about eight- and nine-digit litigation outcomes announced regularly from the late '90s until 2011. VC portfolio companies were often in the crosshairs of patent litigation, finding their own portfolio companies on the wrong end of patent litigation. But the VCs put too much trust in the authors of the AIA bill, and did not realize the harm that would come in the years to follow.

Due to the AIA's patent invalidation feature, VCs have lost a means of financial recovery, and failing VC-backed portfolio companies that cannot pivot (or fail at pivoting) are almost entirely unsalvageable. This makes VC investment like a batter in a baseball game that can only hit home runs or strike out. There is very little in-between. Since nearly 70 percent to 90 percent of VC portfolio companies fail, the one that makes it has to be a home run return to make up for the total loss from the others. With boom-and-bust economic cycles, the need to experience exceptional performance when times are good is heightened because, during the down cycles, VC portfolio companies' difficulties will be heightened, as we have seen in the more recent economic downturns.

On the other hand, the paths for early-stage companies can vary significantly, and the importance of legally protected IP, such as patents, is critical only in specific circumstances. For example, patent protection remains crucial for investment in pharmaceutical, biopharma, and medical device companies (despite the problems Theranos experienced). Products and devices invented in these industries offer stronger patent protection because the stack of patent technology is lower, with few to no work-around options. The patent claims for a drug, diagnostic, or therapeutic are typically covered by a small patent set, which drives massive sales and, therefore, makes infringement easier to detect. As a result, these industries have small patent portfolios that hold exceptional value.

In other industries, such as software, semiconductors, consumer electronics, cloud computing, telecom, networking, cybersecurity, and others, patent protection is often regarded as an afterthought that can be solved later. Other people's patents are often considered a roadblock to innovation, which is a false notion that requires significantly more research and study to debunk (Brandolini's Law). For large industry players in these markets, patents are the antithesis of productive operating companies. However, the weakening of the US patent system has had dire unintentional consequences, which have been lost on the anti-patent advocates who continue to cry foul when patent owners enforce their patent rights. In the dichotomy of pro-patent and anti-patent market participants, the anti-patent enthusiasts have been winning the long-term war over patent rights.

But what if startups did not have to be a complete investment loss upon failure? What if there was an economic system where important intangible assets like patents could provide recovery value to investors? Could it be possible that a failed startup's R&D could be recycled, be reused, and accelerate a new company and/or incumbent's technology plan?

In a bankruptcy setting, the means of recovering lost investment from infringers of IP is often misunderstood, under-reported, and under-recognized by the court system. In the past, countless numbers of failed companies turned to IP for recovery, but that number is now diminishing. Undoubtedly, a VC would rather have a 25 percent recovery from a failed portfolio company than a total loss of investment. Spread that across multiple portfolio companies, and the recovery is meaningful. Moreover, the initial investments into technology and patents for new startups may be reduced since R&D expenses go down when recycling another person's inventive patents. That cannot happen without a stronger patent system.

There is incredible capitalist dogma about how startup value is created and the pricing mechanics behind it, and it is often misplaced. Many VCs that got caught up in the efforts to support the AIA did so because they thought it would help their portfolio companies, not realizing the long-term implications of a weaker patent system. Accordingly, VCs should (but may not) start reversing their support of anti-patent efforts and organizations.

To build a robust economy where "singles and doubles" are considered good investments in a startup, companies need more time and *investment* to build meaningful technology IP that will be adopted in the marketplace. It also means they need the protection of patents to provide operational leverage from larger incumbents entering the same market. Moreover, new and different forms of investment recovery need to be built into a VC's return on investment calculation.

Over the last twenty years, startups have done best when they go viral, which helps build large user bases that are then converted into revenue. Virality is the catalyst that launches unicorn startups. Unfortunately, virality is a fleeting version of technology development that runs counter to exceptional technology creation that stands the test of time. Patents are supposed to be the asset that distinguishes fleeting viral technology versus foundational technology. Unfortunately, the legislative changes under the AIA have had a perverse and confusing effect on the entire patent system, creating exceptional divisiveness between Inventors and Implementers. In the middle are investors who do not understand how to value and price the IP their portfolio companies have created.

TRANSACTING PATENT ASSETS OF FAILED STARTUPS

With failure rates for early-stage companies reaching nearly 90 percent, the need to sell patents out of bankruptcy or failure has grown significantly. I do not track the number of inbound calls from small and individual patent holders looking for investment recovery after their business has ceased operations, but it is a frequent occurrence. Often, the patented IP has no value because no one is using it; nevertheless, I will usually take the call and examine the patent portfolio at a high level before making a decision to work with the patent holder, or not. Sadly, most patent portfolios I review are not worth the effort, time, or expense to value. Repeatedly, I have to tell patent holders that their patents are worthless. Not only that, but they are so worthless that I will not even take your money to try to value the patent. It is not fair to you or me to charge you $5,000 to $10,000 to say, "Your baby [patent] is ugly."

In some cases, where we find infringers of the failed company's patents, there is value to be achieved. Patents that a third party is using are often determined by bringing in subject-matter experts and litigation attorneys to review the portfolio. However, the risk of invalidation can change the fortunes of a patent we believe to carry meaningful value, since the PTAB's IPR may invalidate it.

The impact is a patent transaction market that is an opaque mess of hearsay, private (unavailable) transaction data, scrubbed media reports, or extremely loose comparability from a relatively smaller number of public IP transactions. Said differently, transparency in pricing for patent and IP assets is nearly nonexistent, rudimentary, and generally has bad comparability. Despite tens of thousands of IP transactions or licensing deals occurring yearly, most of those transactions are kept private (and most are intercompany transactions of MNEs). Absent meaningful comparable pricing data, investors in IP and patent assets are left in the dark unless they are extremely sophisticated and experienced in the transaction and licensing of patents and IP.

Unlike real estate, which requires public disclosure of transaction data to aid in pricing discovery and negotiations for other transactions, the patent and IP markets use confidential measures to conceal pricing terms. Regulators often assume that IP data must remain confidential and sealed from public disclosure after a transaction, which allows for asymmetric pricing between large and small entities. While confidentiality of IP transactions is a reasonable precaution, the lack of anonymized IP transaction data creates pricing confusion, which enables "efficient infringement."

With an opaque IP transaction market for selling or licensing, selling IP assets from defunct startup companies has become increasingly difficult to impossible. Moreover, the selling of failed startup company IP assets misses the most important aspect of IP protection for early-stage companies: preventing others from using the patent holder's claims without authorization.

Most of the failed founders I have met over the last twenty-five years have a variety of reasons for their failure. Poor execution, lack of funding, too early to the market, limited product market fit, or any other varied reason that causes failure. More frequently, the refrain I hear from startups is, "A Big Tech company decided to enter the market, and they priced me out while using my technology." It is in those exact situations where the failure of a startup can be directly linked to the actions of a deeper-pocketed competitor where the startup's IP rights are being trampled.

So, how should VCs approach dealing with a weakened

IP system that is undermining investment recovery in failing portfolio companies? First is recognizing the unique difficulties of having a "pivot" strategy as the primary means to assist a failing company. The second would be to advocate a return to a stronger IP system that pushes back on Big Tech encroachment on early-stage company invention and innovation. Doing so would allow for VC portfolio companies to critically invest in IP protection that will legitimately prevent unauthorized use, or will allow for quick and reasonable licensing.

When VC-backed companies invest in companies with patents, they will need to critically evaluate the following:

- presence of patent prosecutors who understand the company's product and market,
- deep and extensive prior art search that can withstand a secondary round of prior art scrutiny that comes with enforcement, and
- the ability to write patent claims in the "goldilocks" zone of claim language.
- To that last point of evaluation, written patent claims are strongest when they are:
- broad enough to be widely used or adopted, but not so broad as to become invalidated,
- not so narrow that it is easy to design around, and
- crafted to find that "just right" level of patent claim.

Confusion and disagreement run rampant within the patent community on what constitutes strong and meaningful patents. It is a debate fueled by anti-patent advocates that believe the entire patent system is unnecessary in modern times (Tabarrok Curve). Influential money provided by Big Tech is often funneled into massive university studies that ultimately shape and influence policy.

Take, for example, Professor Colleen Chien of the University of California. For several years from the late 2000s through the early 2010s, Professor Chien wrote several papers on patents and the issues surrounding patent litigation. Professors from Stanford University, Utah University, and others accompanied her in writing paper after paper about the harm patents had on the startup community. These white papers were passed through the halls of Congress, and a bipartisan agreement was quickly reached that patents harmed innovation.

After the AIA passed, Professor Chien stopped nearly all research on patents, and instead began focusing on other topics like diversity. It is not a coincidence that her focus on patents ended once the AIA became law. Reflecting on the post-AIA outcomes seems like a natural evolution of study unless the original studies were funded with an agenda to help Big Tech.

A LEVEL PLAYING FIELD THROUGH
FINANCIALIZATION OF THE US PATENT SYSTEM

Now, imagine a future patent system that is predictable, robust, stable, and liquid. Early-stage companies that invest in patents but fail to execute or pivot have an IP technology asset that could be adopted and paid for by a third party. The original investor in the failed company has recourse and recovery options available to it, and the buyer of the patented technology receives freedom to operate and the ability to block others from use.

While a scenario like this would be the best possible outcome for many market participants, the system was redesigned under the AIA to limit such scenarios. Under the guise of protecting early-stage companies from patent trolls, the AIA's unintended consequences have made patented IP protection less relevant, more expensive, and generally unhelpful.

If the patent system was strong, however, the process would be smooth and consistent, resulting in low invalidation because the initial patent prosecution efforts would be strong enough to withstand public scrutiny. There would also be a post-grant review process of external validation which already exists but is underutilized. Deputy Director Coke Morgan Stewart has pushed for PGRs to be the primary way for third parties to check the validity of a patent after its issuance. Once IPRs become rare, and PGRs are more frequently used, the "Born Strong" concept of patent applications will create patents that will not be invalidated after they are granted. This should lead to good faith in licensing of patents more frequently by Implementers, creating a transparent licensing market.

Instead of the misunderstood three-step patent prosecution process of "invent, apply, grant," patents should follow a more traditional technology R&D process, followed by an adoption process that adds factors that would produce more harmonious interactions between Inventors and Implementers. To understand why the interactions between Inventors and Implementers are so toxic, sit with any individual or small company Inventor, and the acrimony and frustration are palpable. The promise of patents for Inventors who have lost their IP through the PTAB paints a picture of shattered dreams. It is a nightmare outcome after years of effort, resources, and capital lost in the outcomes of the IPR process.

This is investor hell. When a patented invention of a small company cannot be counted on to protect against infringement, the worst possible outcome is invalidated patents.

There has to be a better way. One that equals the playing

field for Inventors against the regulatory capture that has allowed the largest Implementers in the US to take without compensation to the patent owner. That better way is through better market transparency.

RECYCLING INVENTION AND INNOVATION

Creating a startup company is a monumental undertaking. For many, it is the same as building a rocket ship. The time, effort, and expense required are herculean, and every founder will tell you it was the hardest thing they have ever done. Sadly, the outcome for most startups is a crash into the ground.

Startups repeatedly fail to launch, resulting in a total loss of capital. If our success rates with startups transcended to actual rocket ships, governments worldwide would halt rocket ship building for good. The failure rates would be too high. Yet thousands of startups are created in garages or basements or offices all the time in the US. And our governments encourage it, and highlight the benefits of startup creations as being the biggest job creator in the country, which is true.

But the success of startups past the seed-funding rounds is abysmal. Nearly 90 percent of pre-seed and seed startup companies fail to commercialize a product, which makes receiving a Series A funding round nearly impossible. The table below highlights the material drop-off of companies receiving seed versus Series A funding rounds:

Funding Rounds by Startup Round

VC Stage	Total Companies	Investment Level
Angel/Pre-Seed	1,429	$4
Seed	5,297	$5
Series A	757	$280
Series B	409	$850
Series C	322	$1,048
Series D	266	$1,432
Series E	175	$2,881

Why are seed companies failing to raise Series A capital?

Investment level is the average investment amount in millions of dollars.

Figure 18: Charting the funding rounds of startups by investment stage

For individual and small startups, the time frame between seed funding and the Series A funding round is called the "Startup Death Valley," and it is where MVPs (minimum viable products), PoCs (proofs of concept), and scaling plans go to die.

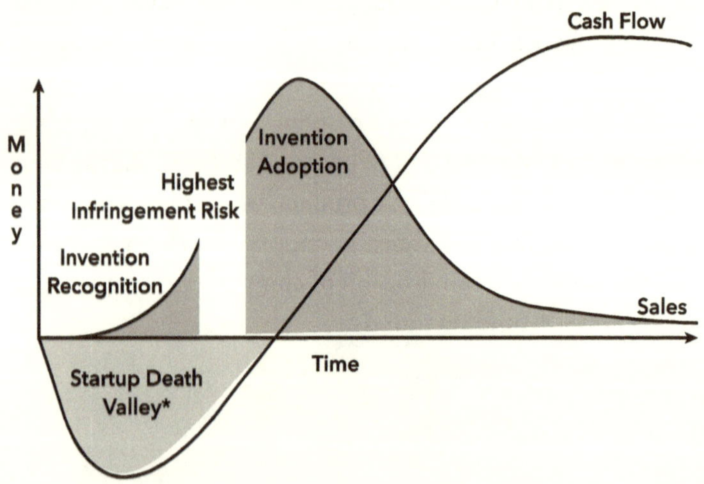

*Refer to "Startup Death Valley Life Cycle" graphic

Figure 19: Startup Death Valley Illustration

The chasm in the time sequence is a standard, unavoidable hazard for startup companies. Financing capital is the lifeblood of startups, and without it companies fail at extraordinary rates. Because failure rates occur regularly for startups, initial investments into seed rounds are much lower than Series A funding rounds, where revenue generation starts to be recurring.

It is during a startup's time in the Death Valley that the initial creation of foundational IP, technology, and patents occurs. Fundamentally, the creation of IP and technology for startups is akin to infancy, and two distinct and separate things are created: a company and its IP. However, most business practitioners do not see or understand the distinction between a company and its IP, making it difficult to separate them. Why is that?

The quick answer is that the US accounting system for tracking, analyzing, utilizing, and pricing IP assets is woefully inadequate. Internally generated IP assets are not expected to be placed on an organization's balance sheet. Instead, a series of amortization schedules are developed to smooth out R&D investment costs, which have no bearing and provide little insight into the developed IP's strength, veracity, or capabilities. Without an initial assessment of value and absent recurring review and understanding of the evolution of the intangible assets' technical abilities, financial impact, and utilization, companies and their advisors are left to value IP assets using arcane methods that are hard to reconcile.

Ask any IP valuation practitioners the most accurate way to value IP assets, and they will agree on the methodologies and approaches, but the outcomes will almost always come out wildly different. Reasonable minds will then disagree, and it requires litigation to determine the IP value, which is never fair "market" value. As a result, IP valuation methods are akin to financial wizardry. Two completely reasonable, objective, and well-intentioned IP valuation professionals can value the exact same IP assets and come up with values that are orders of magnitude different. Examples of IP value differences for the same assets are abundant in the business world. A few real-world examples:

- Nortel Networks's patent portfolio sale during its Chapter 7 bankruptcy: The patents were initially priced at $314 million but ultimately sold for $4.5 billion.
- Trade secrets stolen by employee Anthony Levandowski of Waymo/Google and taken to Uber were initially valued at $2.7 billion, but Uber ultimately paid Waymo $244 million in stock.

These real-world examples of IP valuation and pricing outcome disparities are a small slice of the insanity that exists within IP valuation. The variability and wildly dislocated valuation and pricing mechanisms for IP and technology are literally nonsensical because the system is not set up to treat IP as a real asset. It leaves early-stage investors with one primary strategy: Grow or die.

CHAPTER 8

EVOLVING PATENT STRATEGIES

"In my opinion, there is no 'IP strategy' in this current climate that can override deep pockets, malicious intent, a broken USA enforcement system, or premeditated strategies and budgets for intentional IP infringement and leverage of independent inventors like me."

—JACQUELYN DE JESU, IP ADVOCATE AND
FOUNDER OF SHHHOWERCAP

Racing ideas in his head is a core function of Satoshi's mindset. When he was young, the inventive ideas were a constant barrage of thought and creativity. Finding the ability to channel that energy into creative invention took years to bring into focus. Building mechanical structures was an activity that Satoshi developed early on in his life. The innate curiosity of creatively building was nearly obsessive when Satoshi became a teenager.

Feeling stifled in his home country of Japan, Satoshi's intellectual curiosity and technical prowess led to him to the engineering school at Cal Poly, where his learning curve of mechanical engineering proved incredible. Satoshi's ability to see inventive ideas that improved electronic interactions within computational devices became legendary among his university peers. The ability to find solutions to an advanced technical problem is a unique human quality that many people simply do not possess. Solving technical problems requires an inventive mindset, which Satoshi has in excess.

Because of his amazing aptitude for invention, Satoshi has kept patent prosecuting attorneys busy throughout his professional career. With over three hundred patents in Satoshi's name covering a wide range of electronic devices, Satoshi has become a prolific Inventor. Over the last thirty years, Satoshi's R&D has created nearly five hundred patent applications and his inventions can be found in thousands of products throughout the world. Nearly all of his inventions are being used without his authorization. Due to the challenges with licensing his inventions, he has significantly curtailed his patenting process to include only a handful of his most novel creations. Satoshi's pullback from patenting is representative of a broader issue among Inventors: Efficient infringement is making classic Inventors shy away from sharing their insights and inventions.

THE REALITY OF INVENTION

The patent system has been around for so long that there is a layman's intuitive understanding of how it operates to protect inventions. The basic understanding of the patent system assumes that when an Inventor creates an invention, obtaining a patent will safeguard the technology from third-party use. Unfortunately, nothing could be further from the truth, and the patent strategies that have evolved from the various legislative changes over the centuries will change as widely as the Inventors who seek patent protection from the government.

The process of obtaining a patent is only the first step toward recognizing the value of an invention. Moreover, the inventive process utilized by entrepreneurial Inventors may result in a multitude of patented technology, many times creating patent families through the use of patent continuations. Creating patent families was a time-tested tradition used by patent prosecutors to help limit patent work-around strategies that Implementers have been deploying for decades. However, the practice of patent continuations came under additional threat from the PTAB and USPTO guidance on allowing patent continuations. Fortunately, those plans were abandoned by the outgoing USPTO director, Kathi Vidal, after feedback from market participants.

Nevertheless, the strategies for patent prosecution have been shifting, and a variety of new strategies have been developed over the last few years. Before discussing those ideas, consider what the US patent system is: a repository of technical claims that are easily viewed and often incorporated by third parties into their own products and services. The third parties that adopt the patented technology may do it wittingly or unwittingly, depending on the Implementer.

Good-faith Implementers that created highly technical products will often conduct a freedom to operate (FTO) study to help determine how many patents are being utilized within the product being launched. The number of patents contained inside a product often varies. For pharmaceutical companies, there are usually a small number of patents in a product. But for electronics, like televisions, speakers, or game systems, there may be a few hundred patented technologies included. Then, for even higher tech items like computers, cellular phones, and advanced medical devices (e.g., MRIs or ultrasound machines), there are tens of thousands, if not hundreds of thousands, of patents that go into the device. A high-quality FTO analysis identifies and classifies the patents used in a product into four groups:

1. Owned patents
2. Third-party patents
3. Off-patent or expired patents
4. Indemnified patents (as provided by suppliers)

The technical complexity of the Implementer's product determines the IP strategies of the Implementer. While the ultimate goal for a commercializing entity is to make the highest gross margin, the more complex a product's technology build-out, the higher the likelihood of patent infringement. For high-tech products that are using thousands of patents, the most utilized strategy is to ignore third-party infringement, and wait until approached for a license instead of proactively seeking a license. The ole "it is better to ask for forgiveness than permission" strategy. Often, the forgiveness comes with the cost of losing a patent litigation, resulting in outsized damages awards to patent holders, at least before the AIA became law.

The AIA, however, turned that strategy completely on its head, making it unnecessary to ask for forgiveness for use by simply suggesting that the patent should not have been issued in the first place. Of course, this strategy runs contrary to the original design of the patent system. For a large segment of Investors and operating companies, the patent system hinders innovation and corporate growth. While the ethical action would be to request a license for use after completing an FTO study, many founders seeking a market for their product do not consider in-licensing IP to be a meaningful commercializing activity. Seeking patent licenses from third parties may hold up product adoption, so they skip that work, and hope the weakened patent system's unreliability will allow the Implementer to forego licensing fees.

WHY DO WE HAVE A PATENT SYSTEM?

The common belief is that the patent system was designed to create transparent techniques and methods for integrating an invention into a product that would enable the Inventor to earn commercial returns for the product it produces. In reality, the patent system is a constitutionally appointed government program. If used correctly, the patent system could be the economic infrastructure meant to promote diversity, equality, and inclusiveness in businesses without turning it into an acronym. By creating protectionism for any civilian Inventor, the government should provide a range of opportunities beyond commercialization. Patents create value that is accrued to Inventors based on merit for creativity. The value can only be realized through the sale and transaction of products or services that incorporate the patented technology, either by the patent owner or by a third-party Implementer.

What was previously unknown and misunderstood at the creation of the US patent system was the convergence of technology into stacks. Technology convergence has "stacks on stacks on stacks" of technology in a product. The stacking technology allows for higher product pricing, and creates better operating margins for the Implementer.

However, when the operating margins of a product are not fully attributed to the corresponding technology implemented, the IP value accrues to the Implementer, even if it does not own the IP it is using in its product. The correct way to solve for this is the Implementer's creation of FTO and EoU studies to reasonably account for the technology incorporated into a product. From there, a more accurate operating margin can be established with reasonable payment for using third-party IP.

Absent a direct link from the underlying patent to a product, an operational grey area is created, and operating margins are overstated in a company's financial statements. Implementers underestimate the liability they create for themselves when they (un)wittingly infringe on a third party's patents. While most companies believe their products do not infringe another's patent, there are only a handful of ways to know if that is true or not. The best, most-tried, and most-true method is an FTO study. If the FTO is done right, and the Implementer's engineering and product design team does its job correctly, the company is cleared of financial and technical obstacles before (or shortly after) its launch. Thus, the company is "free" to produce and sell as many products as possible without the threat of future allegations of IP infringement.

For the Implementer whose product takes off, new versions of the initial product often come with various updated features and technologies, some from the internal R&D group, but more frequently from third-party technology convergence. Should companies be conducting a revised and new FTO study for the next version of the product? Of course. Is that policy followed frequently? It is impossible to know.

If you are in-house IP counsel reading this, you will know where you sit on the spectrum under an FTO. In an ideal situation, the in-house IP counsel and the finance group would coordinate to understand the potential liability associated with using another person or company's patents. The two groups could coordinate for compensation to a third-party patent owner. Understanding the patent liability for Implementers should be easier, cheaper, and quicker than litigation, but the system is not working that way.

APPLE VISION PRO CASE STUDY

There is a spectrum of quality and importance that a patent brings to a product. Some patents are much more important to a product, while others are a feature. For most patents in a product, it is tertiary to the product's primary function. These three categories of patent importance define how the patent stack in a product should be classified, with a corresponding allocation of royalty to the technology stack. In patent damages terms, this is called "apportionment."

Apportionment is a controversial topic within the patent and IP community. Most IP experts realize that apportionment is a critical input for understanding IP value, but technical, legal, and financial professionals have all failed at understanding or explaining apportionment to judges and juries. The confusion around apportionment is shrouded in purposeful misdirection. For Implementers, apportionment is a means to show how greedy patent owners are in their requests for compensation; however, it is Implementers who have the knowledge and ability to calculate IP royalty apportionment within a product or service most accurately. Who else knows all the types of technology that have been built into a product besides the commercializing entity?

Apple's launch of the augmented reality (AR) headset, the Apple Vision Pro (AVP), is widely purported to have over five thousand patents incorporated into the product prior to its release. Of those five thousand patents in the AVP:

1. Which patents were created or owned by Apple?
2. How many were patents from third parties and had been licensed by Apple?
3. How many patents from third parties are included, but the patent owner has not been compensated?

In a situation like Apple's, the internal IP team at Apple should conduct an FTO study and begin its efforts to remove obstacles that could result in alleged patent infringement claims. Technical product experts who understand patents, patent law, and the underlying technical claims of a patent portfolio will classify and determine the risk factors from a third-party patent holder. From there, the IP teams will devise strategies to offset the potential product liability through a myriad of methods, including:

1. redesign the technology to avoid the use of third-party patents,
2. seek to cross-license patented technology from the Implementer to the third-party patent owner,
3. buy the patent from the owner directly or through a third-party intermediary,
4. license the patent directly, or
5. rely on a third-party licensing group to provide a covenant not-to-sue.

There may be other remedies, too, but these are the most common ways large companies consider handling obstacles found in an FTO study. For all the hazards of using other Inventors' patents, the reporting mechanisms that lead to a clear FTO report are always privately held. This makes determining infringement costs a black box analysis, and the Implementers dismiss or ignore calls for transparency of IP pricing, hiding behind the false cloak of confidentiality. Without transparent pricing discovery for licensing patents, reasonable licensing fees paid by Implementers to Inventors remains elusive on a wide scale.

However, the answers can be figured out faster than ever thanks to AI platforms being developed for patent portfolio mining and EoU analysis. For example, the launch of the IPDefine patent database, out of Japan, has the capacity to align patent claims with product features and technical details in minutes, which had previously taken weeks or months. The product information contained within the IPDefine infringement database comprises every product or service on the web, including the technical details of a product's features and abilities. These details were then compared to the patent claims of every US patent issued that is active.

Using IPDefine's database, a technical review of all patents contained in the AVP indicates that over ten thousand patents can be reasonably traced into the AVP, meaningfully higher than the five thousand patents suggested in various news articles about the AVP. Going deeper, the IPDefine database can specifically search for how many patents Apple owns that are in the AVP, which is suggested to be 318 unique Apple patents that can be mapped as an EoU. That means over ten thousand non-Apple patents are allegedly being used by the AVP.

Assuming that half of the ten thousand patents used in the AVP are indemnified through supplier agreements, we can infer that the five thousand patents Apple claims to be used in the AVP are either being used under license or without authorization. The patent liability would be significant if even half of the five thousand third-party patents are unlicensed.

In the Apple Vision Pro example, a hypothetical technical review with associated IP licensing fees might look something like this:

Implied Royalties for Developed Technology in the Apple Vision Pro

Patent Owner	Patents for AVP (IPDefine)	RR Value Weighting	Developed Tech Royalty Rate	Strategy for FTO
Apple	318	5%	$17.50	Document utilization through claim charts
Third Party's Patents	~2500	3%	$10.50	License through SSOs, defensive aggregators, or cross-licensing
Off-Patent/Expired/Indemnified	~7000	0%	n/a	Highlight off-patent utilization
Unlicensed Patent Liabilities	~600	2%	$7.00	Patent liability to third parties
Apple Trade	n/a	90% combined	$315.00	Implied value of internally generated technology at Apple
Apple Know-How	n/a			
TOTAL	~10,700	100%	10% OR $350.00	Retail price of $3,499 at a 10% royalty for developed technology is $350 per device

Figure 20: Illustrative example of Developed Technology value allocation

In this example of attributing Developed Technology value to the AVP, the Implementer (Apple) decides on a Developed Technology royalty rate for the AVP. For simplicity, I have selected a 10 percent royalty rate applicable to the Developed Technology in the AVP. Normally, these rates are supported through a search of publicly available licensing agreements that are of comparable technology.

Next, based on the patented technology included in the device, I have assigned the patents into four primary groups:

1. Owned by Apple
2. In-licensed from third parties through cross-licensing or indemnifications

3. Off-patent (or expired) technology that is free to use
4. Unlicensed patent liability

Unlicensed patent liability is the largest point of contention between patent owners and Implementers. For large companies like Apple, it is a never-ending dispute with thousands of patent holders.

The final two categories of Developed Technology, trade secrets and implementation know-how, represent the largest portion of technology from Apple's extensive R&D efforts to create the device. In a hypothetical situation where Apple decides to sell the business unit that created AVP through an M&A, the financial reporting efforts to value the Developed Technology in AVP would need to be disclosed for accounting purposes. After conducting a royalty rate search for benchmarking purposes, an estimated royalty rate of 10 percent of the device's retail price appears to be a reasonable rate applicable to the technology used in the product.

Next, a weighted value is assigned to the royalty rate based on Apple's belief and understanding of technology contribution to the AVP. Value weighting assignment of royalties applicable to technology in a product is and has always been a contentious dispute. Assigning the weightings in the manner I have described has typically been antithetical to most IP departments' operating procedures. Despite the description above being the most reasonable and logical way to complete a technology IP apportionment analysis, I have never met an internal IP department that has undertaken an analysis like this. Why will they not make these types of calculations? Because it opens the Implementer (i.e., Apple) to significant financial liability.

In an ideal world, where Apple (or any Implementer) operates in good faith toward third-party IP owners, the operating returns Apple earns provide it with the resources and capital to always have a clean and clear FTO on the new products it launches. Yet Apple and other trillion-dollar companies are regularly and systematically sued for patent infringement. The apportionment analysis I have completed above should give Apple the ability to reserve a portion of income that could or should be paid to third-party patent owners, but yet they will not do it.

In the simplistic example above, the reasonable expectation Apple should have is to pay third-party patent owners a portion of the seven dollars per device sold. If IPDefine's output is accurate for this example, the pro-rata apportionment for third-party patents would be a royalty rate of $0.012 per device (seven dollars divided by six hundred patents).

A more thorough review and detailed analysis could alter the allocations created in this example apportionment, but the base premise builds the foundation for how patented technology can and should be considered during disputes. Historically, this type of analysis is cost prohibitive, time intensive, and incomplete. With the advances in AI technology, however, these calculations are becoming much easier to determine, review, and audit. Moreover, the Implementer's declaration of a product's Developed Technology royalty rate provides licensing royalty rate guardrails when negotiating licensing agreements, but it requires Implementers to acknowledge use of other people's IP, and then to have a willingness to compensate for use.

For decades, determining technology apportionment has been a black box system. Judicial outcomes in patent litigation have attempted to rightsize damages outcomes, but without a starting point for the declared technology royalty rate in a product, Inventors and Implementers are negotiating from completely different perspectives. Patent owners believe the royalty rates are too low. Implementers believe the royalty rates are too high. To bridge the gap, Implementers need to take ownership of technologies they are incorporating into their products, and build out a financial budget for compensating third-party patent owners. The methodology I describe enables that.

It should not come as a surprise that Apple is using many other people's patents. Apple's public persona as a product maker is "wait and see" before launching a product, and the AVP is another example. Years of planning, design, and development are put into a product before Apple launches, yet every time they launch a product, third-party patent holders find technical evidence of infringement. It is a sign of the times because technology is moving faster now than ever, and there are no signs of slowing down. Yet, clearing third-party patent hurdles slows down and creates internal conflict related to a product's launch. An internal IP department's task is to remove those roadblocks, clearing a path toward FTO.

With technology convergence inevitable, the "not invented here" ethos creates a corporate contradiction that has been dismissed and recategorized as patent trolling from any patent holder seeking to license. It is part of a broader effort to create exceptional IP value for an Implementer's internally created IP, particularly as they become an MNE. For large companies over $20 billion in size, IP's highest and best use is tax avoidance.

THE PARALLEL IP WORLD OF TRANSFER PRICING: INTELLECTUAL PROPERTY'S HIGHEST AND BEST USE

As the US patent system has become ineffectual for individuals and small businesses, the value of technology IP has increased considerably. Many observers suggest that the declining use of patented technology has rebalanced itself into trade secret value, the "supposed" opposite side of the coin to patented technology. Trade secrets combine a variety of IP that is meant to be kept from the prying eyes of competitors. Implementers go through a variety of internal steps to safeguard trade secrets: employment confidentiality agreements, digital security, limited access, and other cybersecurity measures.

Trade secrets, however, are not the opposite of patents. Nevertheless, the use of trade secrets inside multinational enterprises has an important secret that is so common it is overlooked. The sad truth is that Developed Technology and trade secrets' highest and best use is tax avoidance.

For MNEs, the ones with operations in all corners of the world, a process called "transfer pricing" is required because MNEs have cross-border transactions that impact how much tax is paid to a country. The Big Four accounting firms have specialized international tax groups that focus on using internally created IP assets to help lower an MNE's global tax payments by using an "arm's length standard" for charging similar services offered to its sister companies as well as third parties. While this sounds fair and reasonable in theory, MNE companies have figured out how to reduce their global tax rates by selling internally created IP development from high-tax jurisdictions to low-tax jurisdictions.

MNEs do this by moving internally created IP assets into low-tax jurisdictions at the IP's earliest creation (while the value is low) to places like Ireland, the Cayman Islands, or Luxembourg. Once the IP is owned by the MNE in those locations, the company will charge the higher tax locations for the use of the IP, which gets paid to the IP holding company in those low-tax locations.

The result is that the MNE maintains high margins in low-tax areas and incredibly low margins in high-tax jurisdictions, thereby increasing its global profits through tax avoidance. It is a profit-shifting scheme that the Organisation for Economic Co-operation and Development (OECD) uses in collaboration with hundreds of countries to ensure all countries receive their "proper" taxes. However, anyone who looks at the effective tax rates of the largest MNEs knows that it is not working properly. Large companies game the system, and countries throughout the world are receiving less than their fair share of taxable income. It is why large companies' effective tax rates are in the single digits, including huge companies like Apple, Amazon, Google, General Motors, Caterpillar, Coke, Starbucks, and many others.

Every tax season, watchdog groups publish the effective tax rates of the largest companies in the world. Each massive company with global operations uses similar strategies to lower its taxes, and IP assets are at the center of the scheme. To enable these advantages, internally generated IP assets that contain trade secrets, distribution rights, manufacturing know-how, and other "soft" IP assets are valued using OECD guidelines and principles. The "arm's length" principle attempts to value IP licensing agreements by mimicking how two third parties might negotiate a licensing agreement for those same assets.

Unfortunately, the market for similar third-party licensing is an esoteric black box, where transparency, accuracy, and accountability are nearly nonexistent. Instead, transfer pricing uses a theoretical construct for how it "should be" rather than how it "actually is." Transfer pricing uses highly sophisticated econometric analyses to calculate appropriate returns for the "functions" of certain operations in specific countries. These financial calculations are used to determine the "proper" profit earnings for that country. It is this grey area where transfer pricing flourishes, as shown on the IP tax strategy visual below.

DELOITTE'S IP TAX STRATEGY DOCUMENT

IP is a broad category that includes elements that many people associate with the term—like patents and trade secrets—along with components that some organizations may neglect to consider, such as culture and relationships.

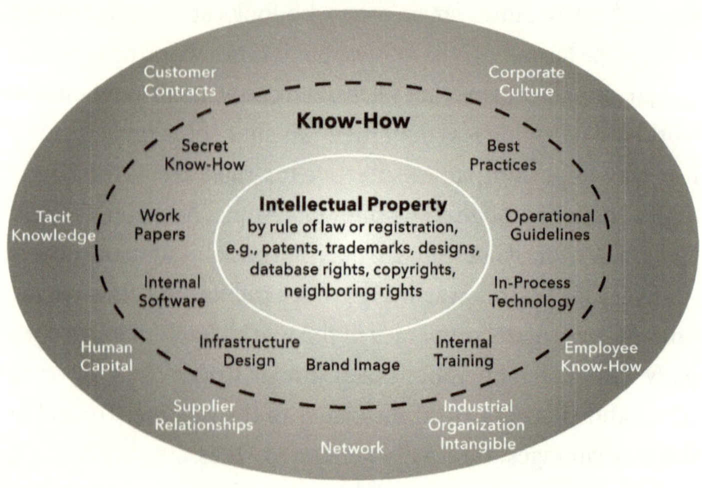

Figure 21: IP's amorphous properties in graphical form

"Free flowing" IP assets within a transfer pricing scheme are the grey area by which profits can easily be apportioned using economic reasoning for profit shifting to various corners of the globe. Taxing authorities that review the IP valuation are usually more concerned with "Is my country getting its right cut of taxable income?" than "Is the IP valuation and process being completed at arm's length?" For this reason, the OECD briefly considered moving from the arm's length standard to a global formulary apportionment standard, which has not been adopted as of this book's publication.

Since transfer pricing is an economic business practice that originated during and after the Second World War, the processes and techniques used are deeply entrenched. Transfer pricing methodologies have changed over the years, but the impact has been superficial and continues to be divorced from reality. Nevertheless, the entrenchment of the transfer pricing practice is so deeply ingrained in MNE business strategy, that the creation of a legitimate third-party licensing and monetization platform would undermine the entire foundation of how transfer pricing operates.

When considering the list of failed private enterprises that have attempted to make IP a financialized platform (i.e., IPXI and IPwe), the least considered reason for the IP platform's failure is transfer pricing. Disrupting the transfer pricing practice that is being used by tens of thousands of companies worldwide is an impossible task without recognizing the inherent influence the practice has on IP valuation and pricing.

If we continue with the Apple Vision Pro headset example, transfer pricing will examine the product's design, manufacturing, assembly, and distribution costs. Then, transfer pricing will optimize the taxes paid across all the jurisdictions where its product will cross borders. For a hypothetical example, the AVP headset will be designed in California, manufactured in China, assembled in Vietnam, packaged in India, and then shipped to its final destination. Transfer pricing's job is to create the lowest possible taxable expense for Apple in each of those countries doing the "low value-add" work, while simultaneously figuring out how to license "internally generated" IP that was created in other locations, like the US or Ireland. The taxing authorities of countries where the work is being completed will insist they receive their share of taxable income, with limited concern about the broader implications of profit shifting to other locations. Tax collectors who receive meaningful jobs programs and income from an international operation are not inclined to be upset about operating profits elsewhere.

The optimization of an effective tax rate for Apple (or a similar large company) is typically arranged with various taxing authorities in an "advanced pricing arrangement" or APA. Countries like to know how much taxable income they will receive, and MNEs do not like surprise tax bills. Transfer pricing economists employed by Big Four and the various taxing authority representatives will meet before a major investment or tax change to negotiate fair payments in advance of a product's launch. Somewhat like a "freedom to operate" analysis but for taxes.

These multilateral discussions between MNEs and the taxing authorities enable the operation of manufacturing and distribution supply chains, the costs associated with those functions, and the appropriate profits for each location. The profits will then determine the taxes paid or received. It is a process designed to create order and allocate taxes through various tax agreements. The transfer pricing studies will also explain how to value marketing and sales operations in the countries delivering the final products at the end of the supply chain. By the end of the APA, a systematic value-chain map with expected pricing and profitability estimates are forecasted and agreed upon.

In the subsequent years, the actual results of the MNE compared to the APA's previous projections are compared, and adjusted according to the APA's terms. Each country with operations in the production chain will receive its tax income in accordance with the APA, and the IP royalties or "excess" profits saved through the APA's mechanisms will be moved and held in the low-tax jurisdiction. Since the financial analyses have been calculated, and determined in collaboration with PhD economists, the operational profits divided between countries and functions are presumed to be economically sound.

While the practice of transfer pricing operates under an arm's length standard, the reality is IP owners are treated wildly different depending on the circumstance. Transfer pricing, as a whole, operates in a vacuum of best practices, and accordingly places extraordinary value on internally generated IP while ignoring the actual difficulties of third-party licensing. It is a corporate paradox that is broadly ignored by regulators and taxing authorities.

What I am saying about transfer pricing may certainly be dismissed by the practitioners who operate in this space. Transfer pricing is a highly complex field and requires professionals with PhDs in economics to administer the plans. While I was working at PwC in the Chicago Transfer Pricing Group, nearly every professional within the practice had a master's degree or higher. It is a practice that relies on highly specialized economists who can rationalize the schemes so that all tax-receiving parties feel comfortable that the local government is receiving its rightful tax income.

The outcomes of transfer pricing schemes tell a different story, however.

Examples of transfer pricing abuses to avoid taxes run rampant in media reports. In 2020, ProPublica published a damning report of Microsoft's transfer pricing abuse in Puerto Rico which helped Microsoft shift over $39 billion in profits to the small island country to the detriment of the US taxpayers. When reporters asked about the scheme, Microsoft responded by saying it "follows the law and has always fully paid the taxes it owes."

However, if a third party had approached Microsoft to license the same IP developed *internally* in Puerto Rico, would

Microsoft have been willing to in-license the IP at the same pricing levels? Not a chance. Anyone who suggests otherwise should be laughed out of the room, but since it was an internally generated IP asset, the intercompany licensing values are orders of magnitude larger and easier to facilitate than had it been a third party with similar IP.

More recently, the European Union has been cracking down on transfer pricing schemes set up by Apple and Google, and the EU has levied billions in fines. The great irony, of course, is that the IP valuation methods that MNEs use to value their own internally generated IP are the same methodologies used to value a third party's IP. The primary difference, however, is the bar for determining IP quality and validity. For most MNEs, internally generated intangibles are of great value, while other people's IP likely is not valid. That is the dislocated problem with the arm's length standards that transfer pricing espouses.

In my experience, and through extensive conversations with a broad range of IP professionals, product design teams, and technical advisors, the best patent strategy for companies is creating a family of patents that protect the primary technical components of a product the Implementer is building. The handful of defining technical features of the product that could be reverse engineered, if not patented, should lead the patent prosecution strategy. These patents become the crown jewels of the patent portfolio because the patented technology on an Implementer's product is the critical feature of the product.

It is at this point in the product creation process that an Inventor/Implementer can begin thinking about patenting in the technical white space around the product, so that the moat of their patent technology is widened. These "white space" patenting strategies by Implementers is how and why there are such a large number of patents issued that are never used.

For decades, large technology firms, such as Nokia, Ericsson, Qualcomm, Texas Instruments, IBM, Intel, GlobalFoundries, etc., designed strategies of their patent portfolios to protect as much technical space as they could. These types of strategies result in invention that begets invention.

Since the AIA, however, patenting into the white space has become much more challenging. White space patenting creates patents that are unlikely to be commercialized by the patentee, but rather used as a preventative measure to exclude work-arounds of the primary patents that cover the featured technology. White space patenting was the go-to patent strategy for most large firms from the late 1980s through the early 2010s. White space patents were often the patents large companies with excess patents would look to for monetization purposes. Patent trolls made their mark on the patent industry by cheaply buying white space patents and then asserting those patents against alleged infringers. White space patents are often tertiary patents to a product's technical purpose, and the enforcement of those types of patents should be transparently acknowledged as such. What should not happen, however, is the blanket invalidation of such patents.

After the AIA became the law, however, these white space patents that were frequently used by patent trolls in enforcement campaigns became the first to be invalidated. These "continuation" patents became the scapegoat of a broken patent litigation system. The shift in policy materially altered patent prosecution strategies for continuations, and in the current environment for patents, companies must find the "Goldilocks Zone" of patent prosecution versus patent ownership versus in-licensing third-party patents as Implementers. It is a delicate task of IP and patent management strategy.

The rightsizing of patent strategy at large companies continues to be a work in progress. As the regulatory fight over patent strength versus weakness continues to play out in legislatures across the world, the technology available to analyze and understand patents continues to improve at a remarkable rate. The wide variety of tools, such as AI patent drafting, AI portfolio mining, blockchain registrations, and other critical technologies, will enable faster and better analysis of large portfolios.

As these IP service programs improve, the market for IP and patent monetization will become easier and faster. Of course, that assumes that Implementers will operate in good faith, and hold respect for other people's patented technology.

In reality, however, most IP departments in companies with a value over $20 billion maintain intransigence toward inventive third parties' patents, and they will use AI tools to undermine IP value of third parties. AI techniques, such as prior art searching and other invalidity efforts, are part of a broader culture of *not invented here*, which is an unstated philosophy of most Implementers accused of patent infringement.

Said differently, AI tools related to patents are a double-edged sword that are wielded in the fight over legally protected IP assets in varied and different ways. That is why the government, in collaboration with IP stakeholders, needs to find the right level of financial fairness with IP assets.

CHAPTER 9

THE DOUBLE-EDGED SWORD OF IP ATTORNEYS

"What do you call a thousand [corporate IP] lawyers chained together at the bottom of the ocean? A good start."

—ANDREW BECKETT, *PHILADELPHIA*, PLAYED BY TOM HANKS

DAVID VS. GOLIATH PATENT BATTLES

For Satoshi Noda, his patents have often been a burden in navigating the technology he owns. It should not be that way, but the AIA has impaired patent ownership for individuals like Satoshi.

"The best technology doesn't always win out," Satoshi explained during one of our weekly calls. "Or it does, but the right people don't get the credit for its invention."

"What do you mean by that?" I asked.

"Building technology to scale fast creates companies with weaker fundamental technology. It is like building a house. Do you want a house constructed faster than reasonable so the buyer can move in? Or do you want it done well, and up to a specific regulatory code? I'd probably think the latter. In that way, patents help Inventors demonstrate their best-invented method, but the 'build fast and break things' model places value on speed over quality. It helps build large user bases, but eventually they have to adopt better technology that infringes our patents, so we have to litigate our patents because we worked hard on solving the technical problem. While others worked hard on building a user base, they neglected the technology, so now they need to work around our patents or take a license."

"Until they get big enough to not care that they are using it, and decide to take it and pretend they've worked around it," I responded.

"And that is why we need litigation funding," Satoshi said.

Satoshi is one of the smartest, savviest Inventors I have met, but I am not the only one who recognized his inventive genius. His investors saw in the early 2000s that they were investing in Satoshi as an Inventor for the long term. Unfortunately, the patent portfolio he built starting in 2004 was developed under a system that has almost entirely changed after the AIA. The inventions and innovations Satoshi has created should have ushered in fantastic wealth with multiple businesses. Instead, he has had to rely on repeatedly pivoting his business while seeking litigation funding to support recourse for massive and widespread infringement of his patented technology. While his patents chart a path for at least seven or eight different startups ranging from banking technology to cybersecurity to device payment systems, Satoshi's patented technology represents foundational technology that should usher in the future of commercialized digital commerce. Instead, Satoshi is embroiled in a series of patent litigations that are decades in the making.

Satoshi is one of the "lucky" patent owners, too. The patent enforcement agents in this incredibly strict and tight environment for patent litigation know a good patent when they see one. Patent litigators and litigation funders conduct extensive due diligence on patents before they decide to invest in patent litigation, and Satoshi has built an armory of patents. Subject matter experts have completed an extensive review of his patents, and the claims should win in litigation, except for the PTAB risk, which considerably heightens the potential for invalidity findings.

The gauntlet a patent holder goes through when enforcing against an infringer has never been harder in the US. The standard for litigation has been raised to a level that can seem overwhelming to overcome. The stages of trials and tribulation that a patent holder goes through upon identifying an infringer of its IP is overwhelmingly challenging, extraordinarily costly, and there is a low probability of success.

Satoshi's and Ray Yarris's invention and innovation stories paint a picture of harrowing backlash from a business environment replete with soft copying, sometimes even brazen copying. A reasonable response to the copying should be compensation, but the US legal system is often too slow to help early-stage companies, and so the startup companies fail. Those failed companies' patents often fell into the hands of patent trolls during the heights of the patent troll era from the late 1990s until late 2011. Once the AIA took hold, however, patent holders were sieged by a series of efforts to undermine the patent system.

For Satoshi, Ray, and thousands of other patent holders, their patents should have provided them protection or income, but instead, the patent system has repeatedly delayed or denied justice through a slow and tedious legal byzantine. Despite gaining meaningful market traction through commercialization, the weak patent system has stymied their opportunity for justice against infringement through delays, obfuscation, and invalidation efforts.

Buried in the rubble of the imploding patent system for individual Inventors is the technology necessary to build a robust IP financial system that can be digitized, streamlined, and built for fair business dealings. If put into place, stories like Ray's and Satoshi's would shift from pain and trauma to great success and financial reward for having their patent technology openly adopted into products and services.

Strong, useful, and protective patents are built upon three distinct foundations: legal, technical, and financial support. The Venn diagram below highlights a commonly held belief by patent practitioners that patents are built on these pillars. The overlap among these practices is where the strongest patents hold and maintain value.

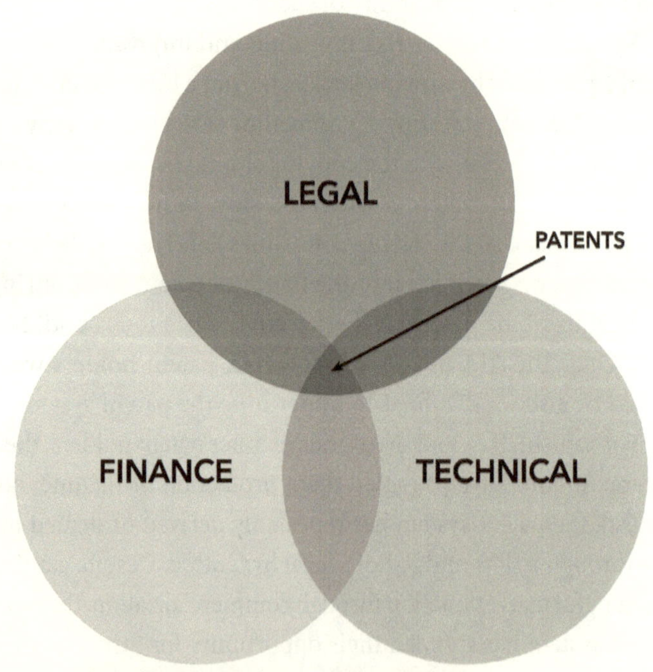

Figure 22: A Venn diagram of the most valuable patented technology

At least, this is what I thought for many years while practicing IP valuation. I have come to understand that those three factors have been undermined by political support from large enterprises that received help from the government that enacts patent laws. These laws have been tilted in favor of the largest companies. The willingness of bipartisan politicians to rebuild the patent system to benefit the largest and deepest-pocketed companies has eroded good-faith individual Inventors and small companies. The lobbying of politicians has unquestionably created the weakest patent system in the US since the 1970s, and despite those changes, IP attorneys continue to do well whether the patent system is tilted toward strength or weakness.

Despite society undergoing the most significant technological change in history the last thirty years, leading to the vast sums of wealth created by enterprises, the average value of patent portfolios has moved materially lower than prior to the AIA's enactment. Moreover, technical discoveries made by competing Inventors during simultaneous or tangential invention sessions result in overlapping technology that is often used as a way to invalidate patents after the patents were granted. While technology advances rapidly, the patent system is underdeveloped to keep pace with these changes.

MOVE ~~FAST~~ SLOW AND BREAK THINGS

The pace of innovation is moving faster than ever, but the patent system and the legal system that backs it move at a glacial pace. Patent pendency, the time it takes for an application to become a granted patent, is at its slowest in modern history, and is finally getting better. Examiners of patent applications are overworked and underappreciated. The pressure on examiners has led to low morale among the entire USPTO.

Examiners are under significant pressure to "get things right," and the fear of seeing their work undone in a post-tribunal IPR process only adds to their burden. To commiserate, patent examiners have taken to Reddit to complain about their problems. Patent examiners are under attack, and the USPTO leadership has had problems providing useful guidance to patent examiners. For patentees, this increases prosecution expenses. Moreover, it does not limit the potential of post-grant invalidation procedures.

Thankfully, the new USPTO leadership is de-emphasizing the IPR process in favor of post-grant review (PGR) procedures, which allow for the public to challenge a patent's validity within the first nine months of its issuance. Further, Director Squires and Deputy Director Stewart have made meaningful use of discretionary denials at the PTAB's IPR under a doctrine of settled expectations. By time-barring when a patent can be instituted for IPR, the expectation that alleged infringers can and should pay reasonable licensing fees to patent owners becomes more likely. The collective changes from Squires and Stewart have renewed optimism for small company and individual Inventors for the first time in a decade.

Slower initial examination times are only the start of problems with the patent system, however. A bevy of anti-patent organizations continue their relentless efforts to further weaken the patent system.

Take the LOT (License on Transfer) Network as an example. It was founded by a consortium of Big Tech companies in 2014, with the goal of reducing patent litigation. The organization's mission is to protect companies from unwanted patent litigation, and every member that joins commits to a non-patent assertion policy if or when its members go through a transaction process—any company or investment transaction process. In effect, the LOT Network pledge is that if a company is acquired through M&A, all the other members receive a pledge that the buying entity will not subject LOT members to future patent litigation by the buyer.

It blunts a patent's effectiveness in preventing unauthorized use. By providing blanket non-assertion pledges, it effectively gives permission to LOT members to use the patent without payment. While the LOT network promotes that members "can still sue for infringement," the reality is, intermember patent litigation is a rare occurrence. Said differently, the entire organization is designed to weaken patent rights.

In 2018, I was invited to attend the LOT Network annual conference at the Palace Hotel in San Francisco. I have attended countless IP conferences in my career, but this one was unique. The largest companies in the world gathered at the posh hotel to discuss ways to invalidate patents when third parties assert their rights in court. Session after session was led by panelists who had "survived patent trolls." The panelists described detailed methods that have worked at the PTAB to invalidate patents. It was a disheartening conference to attend, and one I am glad I will never have to attend again. The attendees were literally giddy at the prospect of invalidating patents. It was a joy for the attendees to teach and learn from each other about patent invalidation techniques. I found it gross.

Sadly, the number of small company members attending the LOT Network conference was a fraction of the numerous attendees from large organizations and the massive law firms that helped them evade patent licensing fees. Not one session would have been useful to early-stage companies looking to create a protective moat around products and services to protect against the predatory efforts of Big Tech. Helping small companies to work with Big Tech to in-license IP was not part of the scene.

Since attending that conference, I have dubbed the LOT Network a "league of serial infringers." Companies that join the LOT Network do so because they either plan to infringe another Inventor's patented technology or already are infringing. Rather than helping create a marketplace to assist other Inventors, they have created a cabal of like-minded infringers whose primary purpose is to undermine patents.

Next is the "defensive patent aggregators." There are two main organizations here: RPX Corporation (RPX) and Allied Security Trust (AST).

RPX, the "rational patent exchange," was founded in 2008 as a reaction to the explosion in patent litigation. The basic premise was to bring together deep-pocketed companies that were being accused of patent infringement and collectively solve the problems each company faced individually. Companies would pay a membership fee to be part of RPX, and RPX would, in turn, buy or license patents as a collective, thereby thwarting patent assertion efforts and spreading the risk. RPX was meant to provide the freedom to operate (FTO) from patent litigation.

For a time, RPX was wildly successful and, at its peak, had a $3 billion market cap value. As a defensive aggregator, RPX was part of the consortium that purchased the Nortel Network patents out of bankruptcy. With a growing need for patent assertion defense, RPX thrived when patents were strong in the late 2000s, but after the AIA was enacted, John Amster, CEO and co-founder of the firm, was one of the few experts calling for a significant retrenchment in the entire patent system.

In 2012, at Ocean Tomo's inaugural economic and financial IP market conference, John was the only featured speaker who distinctly said, "I hate to be a downer, but I think patents are going to have a very difficult time under the new legislation." The other keynote speakers brought a cautiously optimistic view toward the legislative change, expecting that the more recent liquidity that had come to the patent markets was going to transition patents and IP into a meaningful investment asset class. John's pessimistic view of patented IP stood out, not because he was the only one with that view but rather because he was presciently omniscient about the future of patents.

John's view eventually led to meaningful disagreements with RPX's board of directors, as patent values and licensing payments declined precipitously under the AIA. By February 2016, John resigned as CEO of RPX, and the company was eventually taken private. HGGC, the private equity firm that made the investment to buy RPX, paid $555 million for the firm, a steep discount to its highest value of $3 billion five years prior.

RPX's current CEO is Dan McCurdy, the former CEO of the other patent defensive aggregator, Allied Security Trust (AST). Similar to RPX, AST's mission is to reduce patent litigation on behalf of its members, which are typically large, well-funded technology companies. AST, however, is a "nonprofit" and its business model is a "catch-and-release" process. AST and its members work in collaboration to buy patents which pose a threat to its members, license the willing members who need it, and then sell the patents back to the market with the encumbrances intact.

AST uses a patent buying process called IP3, an annual patent buying program designed to provide liquidity to patent holders who want a more sophisticated way of monetizing patents than with the brute (and risky) force of litigation. AST is not in the business of litigating patents, and only makes patent purchases or licenses if the AST members want confidential help resolving its members' patent disputes with third parties.

The IP3 is a program born out of Google's "Patent-Palooza," which Google deployed in 2015 with some success. The basic idea is that any patent holder could submit their patents to Google or AST for any ask price they had in mind. Google (and now AST) would then consider each patent offering on its merits and decide whether to accept the offer, negotiate a lower price, or decline. The initial effort to complete a buying program brought out desperate patent holders looking for liquidity. The inaugural patent buying program run by Google resulted in a meaningful number of offerings being made with asking prices ranging from thousands to billions on request. Google ultimately bought a small percentage of the offerings, but the bigger point was made: Google was trying to make a market for buying patent assets through the program.

After Patent-Palooza, AST adopted the program, renaming it IP3, and continues to run it to this day. While AST's leadership likes to promote the program as a successful means of creating a market for patent sellers, the low purchase-to-offering ratio of less than 10 percent is an abysmal statistic that leaves most patent holders frustrated and without a return on their patents.

Without a doubt, however, the worst actor toward patent holders over the last fifteen years has been a firm called Unified Patents. Founded in 2012, the company is also a membership group with a primary mission to deter patent trolls. To that end, Unified Patents is a prolific filer of IPRs against entities who assert patents in litigation. Their website used to brag about how "we don't monetize transactions by paying. In fact, we never pay. Ever."

To Unified Patents, every patent owner who asserts a patent is a troll. The organization's leadership openly brags on LinkedIn about successful invalidation and mocks patent market participants who dare to defend patent rights. There is no distinction, empathy, or compassion toward patent holders who have lost everything when Unified Patent invalidation efforts succeed. To them, every patent is a bad patent, and none are worth paying a licensing fee for.

Unified Patent's crowdsourcing efforts to invalidate patents highlight the intransigence toward patent holders. The boastful aggression to invalidate every patent it possibly can casts a shadow over the entire patent system because the outcome of invalidation is so devastating to patent holders. Moreover, despite the Government Accountability Office's (GAO) review of the PTAB system finding that 75 percent of Administrative Patent Judges felt pressure to invalidate patents, Unified Patents continues its arrogant and distasteful efforts to throttle patent holders' rights through the IPR process.

Still worse, the Unified Patent team often authors and publishes one-sided studies and reports proclaiming that patent trolls continue their pursuit of "frivolous" patent litigation, despite overwhelming evidence that the patent assertion entities have retrenched. In late 2024, Michelle Aspen of Unified Patents wrote a scathing and wholly inaccurate story in JUVE Patent titled "Fire First, Ask Questions Later: The New Normal of No-Notice Patent Suits," which falsely proclaims that patent holders are suing as an initial opening act of licensing patents rather than engaging in licensing discussions first. While I do not dispute that litigation-first strategies are happening, the number of patent holders I know and have represented engaging in good-faith patent licensing is substantial. In fact, most patent holders I know would rather not engage in patent litigation, but cannot because of the overwhelming actions to invalidate by organizations like Unified Patents.

Standing behind all these organizations is Google, providing funding, advice, and space to continue the relentless effort to undermine the US patent system. Google's influence, sponsorship, and involvement have been necessary to the success of these organizations. In truth, Google is supportive of anti-patent initiatives, and has been a major contributor to advanced patent invalidation efforts. In addition, Google has sponsored the following anti-patent organizations:

- Electronic Frontier Foundation's anti-patent efforts
- Academic studies to undermine patent rights through:
    - University of California-Berkeley (Professor Colleen Chien)
    - Stanford University (Professor Mark Lemley)
    - University of Utah (Professor Jorge Contreras)

It did not stop there, however, because Google's former head of IP, Michelle Lee, was made the director of the USPTO from March 2015 until June 2017. Prior to that, Michelle Lee held the position of deputy general counsel and head of Patent Strategy at Google. It was during this time that Ms. Lee, under the authority of Eric Schmidt (former Google CEO from 2001 to 2011), created the broad plan to transform the US patent system through the financial support of the organizations, academic research, and a public relations campaign that would enable the explicit weakening of the patent system for the direct benefit of Big Tech companies. Undoubtedly, the effort worked better than they could have possibly expected.

On August 15, 2024, Mr. Schmidt was giving a talk to a group at Stanford when he said the quiet parts out loud:

In the example that I gave of the TikTok competitor—and by the way, I was not arguing that you should illegally steal everybody's music—what you would do if you're a Silicon Valley entrepreneur, which hopefully all of you will be, is if it took off, then you'd hire a whole bunch of lawyers to go clean the mess up, right? But if nobody uses your product, it doesn't matter that you stole all the content. And do not quote me.

This extreme position by the former head of Google is unquestionably a tactic he has implemented before. The ramifications of actions like he has described have decimated the US patent system, leaving individual and small company Inventors broke, broken, and dismayed. Meanwhile, Google's market capitalization is above $3 trillion.

The nefariousness of the plan to systematize the use of third-party patented technology without authorization has been decades in the making. It started back in the early 2000s when Eric Schmidt first took over as CEO of Google, and culminated in Michelle Lee's becoming the director of USPTO in 2015 during the time when the PTAB's IPR system was reaching full throttle. The variety of "behind the scenes" actions by Google is a trail of covert anti-patent actions that, when brought together in a collective, represent an egregious effort to undermine the US patent system.

The harms of these collective actions, underwritten and enacted for the benefit of Google and Big Tech, have upended the lives of countless individuals and small Inventors and financially harmed them beyond reason. Applying for a patent was supposed to protect against deep-pocketed infringement. The broad-sweeping efforts to undermine the US patent system through the actions of the largest technology companies in the world have created a lopsided market that is most beneficial to large companies. Regardless of how effectual the efforts to weaken the US patent system have been, there continues to be a strong, well-intentioned group of anti-patent advocates who continue their relentless pursuit of weakening the patent system further.

In this long and ongoing battle between Implementers and Inventors, what is lost in the narrative is the simple notion of compensation for use. Implementers have been using the same arguments and ideas for several decades now, which is that patent owners are the real problem at issue, when in fact it is the Implementers of new technologies that are at issue. Any IP attorney worth his weight would recognize this fact, but it is the ignored elephant in the room in all discussions related to problems that plague the patent industry: serial infringement by large Implementers is unrecognized as a legitimate problem. That was until the new leadership at the USPTO started enacting change.

When large companies are unwilling to recognize the invention of another person and, worse, they go out of their way to destroy the invention through the IPR process, they leave in their wake a trail of sadness and tears that cannot be recovered. Fortunately, Director Squires and Deputy Director Stewart have heard the calls for PTAB reform, and are raising the standard for what should be invalidated through the IPR process.

FIXING THE PATENT SYSTEM

CHAPTER 10

THE GOVERNMENT'S ROLE IN FIXING PATENTS

"Private property is an extremely useful idea—arguably one of our greatest inventions. So far, each new definition of it has brought us increasing material wealth. It seems reasonable to suppose the newest one will too. It would be a disaster if we all had to keep running an obsolete version just because a few powerful people were too lazy to upgrade."

—PAUL GRAHAM, "DEFINING PROPERTY," ESSAY, 2012

CREATING A LEVEL PLAYING FIELD TO SUPPORT INDIVIDUAL AND SMALL BUSINESS INVENTORS

One of the challenges the US gets wrong with Inventors is the alignment of incentives. Take, for example, the USPTO's Patent Pro Bono Program for small businesses and individuals. The base tenet of the service is "free legal assistance in preparing and filing a patent application. The Patent Pro Bono Program is a nationwide network of independently operated regional programs that matches volunteer patent attorneys and agents with financially under resourced inventors and small businesses to provide free legal assistance in securing patent protection."

While I do not take issue with providing free legal assistance to Inventors, it is the underrepresentation of what the true cost of ownership might mean to patent holders. The expense of a patent does not end after the issuance of a patent. The ongoing development of a patent's claims into a business represents one of the most under-invested areas in the US economy.

For all the patents the USPTO issues per year, only a small percentage of those patents become broadly used in commercialized products. The actual figure varies widely by expert, but somewhere between 1 percent and 15 percent of granted patents become utilized in products. An even smaller percentage of those patents are litigated for infringement, and even fewer become meaningful collateral for investment purposes. That means that most US patents carry little to no value, except for the "potential" to be commercialized in the future. In financial terms, that's "option value."

The intuitive economist should recognize that nominal improvements in the USPTO's issuance of "utilized" patents in commercial products would have a meaningful and recognizable impact on the US economy. In fact, the idea of changing patent fees from user fees to valued utilization is part of the forward thinking necessary to bring the US patent system into the twenty-first century. By creating a digitized patent system, the monetization options for IP expand significantly beyond the current iteration of issuance, creating a meaningful platform that equals the playing field for all patent and IP creators and users.

Most patent and IP professionals I know accept the fundamental technology flaws that accompany the patent system.

Conducting twentieth-century legal prosecution and adjudication of patents in the twenty-first century is a travesty of inaction. The US patent system provides support, guidance, and assistance in only two areas: prosecution and litigation. The time between having a patent granted and finding an "alleged" infringer is entirely on the patent owner. The cost, time, and effort needed to protect individual and small company Inventors from large-scale infringement are several orders of magnitude larger than the pro bono services used to prosecute those patents.

If the US government really believes it can provide a tax on patents, it is going to need better mechanisms to enforce patent rights. Right now, most patent owners deserve a refund for being issued an unenforceable asset! Are the legal services being provided to pro bono patent prosecution services teaching individuals and small companies the true cost of enforcing patents that a larger entity might infringe? I doubt it. If they did, no rational Inventor would apply for a patent.

So, what does an "ideal" patent system look like, anyway?

First, it is digital, and all the information related to a patent (or patents) is contained in a single, authoritative agency;

second, pendency for the application and issuance of new patents is done quickly and with the latest technology available (i.e., blockchain and artificial intelligence) in collaboration with human expertise in specific subject matters,

third, granted patents provide a range of options, including

exclusion of use,

fair compensation for use,

confidence in issuance from the government, and

fair, equitable, and quick adjudication of unauthorized use;

fourth, financial options, including

investment,

licensing,

monetization, or

other financial considerations related to IP issuance; and

fifth, financial, technical, and legal alignment of incentives for the promotion, use, and adoption of technology for all stakeholders within the country's economic system.

The IP system's ability to reflect and consider what is needed from the US government to enable a patent system that levels the playing field is an idea well past its time. Time and again, the common refrain from astute individuals operating in the patent space who want a better system is the idea of rebuilding the program from scratch. From Michael Lee (Facebook's head of IP), to Gene Quinn (founder of IPWatchdog), to Erich Spangenberg (renowned patent enforcement agent turned patent system entrepreneur), the consensus is that the patent system is too antiquated.

IP MODERNIZATION

All companies are at risk of unintentionally infringing on another person's or company's patented technology. (Un)wittingly infringing third-party patents is what gave rise to patent trolls, and the unique investing edge of buying patents for enforcement purposes became duplicitous from the late 1990s until the AIA became law. Many argue that patent trolls exploit bad patents that should never have been issued in the first place. These anti-patent sentiments brought forth by the PTAB's IPR process create a double jeopardy validity assessment, with the second validity review occurring after the patent has already been issued.

Moreover, these two validity assessments have inconsistent views in prior art discovery, creating misunderstanding and confusion among patent practitioners. America's patent experts' misunderstanding and disagreement of what constitutes a valid patent has undermined the value of patent portfolios, across the board.

So how do we fix this mess of a process?

First, the USPTO desperately needs modernization. The creation of a patent system is a type of government-controlled platform, and the underlying technology that underpins the USPTO is outdated and difficult to use. The US patent system is critical infrastructure for maintaining a repository of America's best inventions, yet its user interface is awful. The USPTO website looks like it was built in the 1990s and has barely been updated.

Second, embattled patent examiners need to be given more credit, accolades, and resources for the thankless task they perform. Being a patent examiner is an extraordinarily hard job that has exceptional turnover. Moreover, examiners' work is constantly criticized and reviewed by third parties who are trying to find flaws in their process. The third parties are given nearly unlimited time and resources, whereas examiners are on tight timelines with weak resources. Examiners deserve better, and modernizing the system to enable examiners to do their jobs well is vital to improving the health of the patent system.

While there have been efforts to streamline certain aspects of the prosecution and application process, technical glitches have become a norm. These problems have led to a backlog of patent applications that have delayed the examination process. Julie Burke, a former USPTO examiner turned USPTO whistleblower, has been tracking and commenting on the technology deficiencies at the USPTO for several years now.

"The DOCX initiative is, from my point of view, quite problematic for patent practitioners. It seems to be a mechanism for the US Patent and Trademark Office and the patent examiners to more efficiently handle files, but it comes at great cost for document integrity and the integrity of the underlying documents of the patent applications," Burke wrote on LinkedIn.

Moreover, Jeff Lindsay, a patent attorney with global experience from Wisconsin to China, has highlighted the issue of regressive technology within the USPTO, stating on LinkedIn, "What happened with USPTO's software systems and the no-bid contract behind their costly decay merits Congressional investigation and accountability. Such a pain and even danger (relative to IP rights) for many."

Suffice it to say that America's technology center does not match the ingenuity and spark that its Inventors expect or deserve, and it seems to be worsening. Some of the problems are ineptitude, but it is hard to tell if the issues are purposeful or because of ignorance. The impact of a diminished and ineffectual US patent system creates a grey area of dispute by which large, anti-patent groups can exploit the system.

In Jonathan Barnett's book *The Big Steal*, the IP professor highlights how there has been a two-decade effort to weaken IP rights in the US for the benefit of large tech companies:

> What many observers did not seem to appreciate is that a weak-IP environment may simply advantage leading platforms that specialize in the organization and distribution of the otherwise unstructured mass of informational assets that proliferate in digital environments. For Google's search engine, YouTube's video streaming site, and Facebook's newsfeed, content is an input that is required to attract users and, in turn, advertisers. *The platform intermediary rationally seeks to minimize its input costs and pursues that objective by adopting an advocacy strategy designed to weaken IP protections, which lowers the price (often to zero) of acquiring the content that is necessary to attract platform users and advertisers.* (emphasis mine)

The unwinding of IP rights through the weakening of the IP system has had outsized benefits and returns for Big Tech companies, to the detriment of individuals and small businesses. In fact, the slow advancement of patent infrastructure technology places Inventors at a disadvantage to alleged infringers because tracking, monitoring, and enforcing against infringers can be a sizable portion of an internal IP team's job description. Patents that do not prevent third parties from using the claimed technology in the invention are ineffectual. Sophisticated patent holders, regardless of their size, will seek to enforce against unauthorized use whenever it is found, but under the AIA, patent enforcement is unreliable, slow, and a general threat to the validity of the issued patent.

The systematic flaw of the IPR appeal process undermines the reliability of a "valid" issued patent. In fact, it renders patents for most small companies nearly meaningless. To improve the patent system's reliability, the base infrastructure of the patent system needs to provide meaningful insights, utilization statistics, commercialization assistance, pricing discovery, and monetization options. Creating an IP platform capable of financializing IP is a massive undertaking that cannot be done without the government's faithful involvement in creating a balanced system that works for small and individual entities, not just the biggest, deepest-pocketed companies. Technology exists to make it happen, too. However, the USPTO can barely implement the most basic upgrades without encountering technical issues that hinder Inventors.

Blockchain, as an infrastructure database, could provide a foundational structure for vastly improving the patent system into a technological and economic platform. This does not mean the IP system should become a cryptocurrency. Hardly at all. Rather, the blockchain system should be the base tracking, accounting, and operating system of patents and all forms of technology IP, which are a core function of the US and global economic system.

As noted earlier in this book, several private enterprises (i.e., IPXI, IPwe) have attempted to modernize patent licensing platforms, but the systematic flaws are too big for private enterprises to overcome. Moreover, there has been a sustained effort by large technology companies that thrive under a weakened IP regime to maintain the status quo that is necessary to slow justice through regulatory capture. Unless, and until, the regulatory capture that allows serial infringement to occur is recognized and limited, the importance of IP will be ineffectual to huge swathes of small businesses for fear of infringement from massive incumbents.

However, an IP system built with modern, blockchain infrastructure that enables meaningful financial insights and monetization across all the ways IP can be used would be transformative to the economy. If done correctly, the patent system flips from being an exclusionary asset to an enabling asset, where everything does not have to be invented in-house. Rather, a searchable database for enabling foundational IP could be in-licensed by early-stage (or more established) companies at pre-established royalty rates on a royalty base. It is an idea based on asking for permission rather than forgiveness, or worse, invalidating another creator's hard work.

Said differently, a patent blockchain database creates a market where fair compensation for use is the norm. It is an idea far past its time, and one that Implementers would be unwilling to enact because of the historical profiteering that the largest companies in the world will have to eliminate from their operations. The historical status of the patent IP system is a pendulum that swings back and forth over time as political winds change, and that swinging pendulum needs to end. In its place, a level playing field that accurately attributes and compensates technology and patented invention to the right Inventors.

Imagine a system where IP licensing and monetization can happen quickly and enable the best possible technology to be adopted, rather than having private company engineers spending their time designing work-arounds. Instead, imagine that the private company engineers create the best possible solution, and then if or when the use of a third party's patents is recognized, a simple and quick payment for use is made.

To enable and unlock the financial opportunity of quickly licensing patented IP technology, the underlying system needs to be invested into, with an expectation that IP can be financialized into a liquid trading platform. Because IP is a complex asset that has multiple utilities, the financial platform created needs the flexibility to adjust to monetization efforts while simultaneously aligning with existing regulatory and financial accounting procedures. This is where technology and regulatory convergence become the method for transitioning IP into a monetizable platform.

The act of recreating and applying the financial and accounting systems that run the debt and equity markets, but through technology IP assets, is the way companies could and should account for IP on their balance sheets. Moreover, the IP licensing fees earned and paid should run through a company's income statements above the operating profit line.

Under current US accounting laws, internally generated IP assets are not accounted for on a balance sheet. Moreover, IP licensing income or expenses are not accounted for on the income statement in a consistent manner across all companies. The absence of accounting and valuing of patents and IP is the grey area where infringement runs rampant because patented technology enforcement is 100 percent relied upon by the Inventor.

In the modern financial accounting system, regulators utilize a "trust but verify" system, whereby internal accountants create the accounting procedures and financial statements using a standard set of generally accepted accounting procedures called GAAP. Without modern financial accounting, investors in public companies would not trust the financial statements. It is the combination of "trust but verify" accounting that enables a transactable secondary market for equity and debt securities.

Similarly, IP assets that are financialized for early-stage company investment will need a similar "trust but verify" accounting and valuation method that can create a meaningful secondary market for IP financial securities, like IP debt or IP equity. By creating a secondary market for transacting IP securities, benchmarking methods for reconciling value versus price become a meaningful method of accurately assessing the value of IP assets.

Without a meaningful secondary market, assigning value to IP and patent assets is a complex endeavor that often requires information and data that does not exist—or exists but is not disclosed. Understanding and assigning value to IP is incredibly difficult without the disclosure of critical information. Accordingly, the government's role is to create a financial platform for IP rights that can be monetized through the sale, license, or investment in IP assets that will result in simple and consistent disclosure of comparable pricing. And while many would suggest that maintaining confidentiality and privacy will be impossible, I would challenge that theory. Developing an IP financial platform to mimic traditional debt and equity platforms is possible, provided the system recognizes the unique nature of IP assets.

In the Apple Vision Pro example, two simultaneous actions are happening when declaring a "Developed Technology" royalty rate:

- First, the establishment of a specific income stream related to the Developed Technology being incorporated into the device.
- Second, a recognition of the IP integrated into the device from the product creator and from third parties.

The allocation of the declared royalty rate to internally generated IP versus third-party IP creates a two-prong cash flow. One for enabling investment returns to the Implementer and the second to third-party Inventors whose patented IP is being used by Apple. By defining the two cash flows that are attributed to the Implementer and Inventor, creators and Inventors of all types become enabled. Further, the (privately or publicly) declared product royalty rate puts a cap on the cost, which CFOs and controllers can budget for reasonably.

This process can be replicated countless times for any company incorporating technology into its products. Furthermore, by reserving a small portion of royalty income attributable to third-party IP and then allocating it to those third parties on a digital platform, the Implementer can obtain true and legitimate FTO. Through a digitized platform that makes payment for using third-party patents through an automated system created by the government, the ability to pay for alleged infringement becomes materially easier to adjudicate and settle.

The underpinning of all of this are technical and financial accounting standards. Creating financial accounting standards took centuries to develop, and it is constantly evolving to provide investors with better insights into a company's operating performance. In a similar way, a technical accounting of a company's utilized IP and patent assets would provide IP investors with the confidence that a product or service is ethically and morally offering products that are not infringing on another person's IP. Or if the product is using a third party's IP, that corrective action to remove the technology (work-around) or compensate the IP owner is easy. Absent a regulatory framework around the technical accounting for IP assets in a product, systematic abuse and serial infringement run rampant, and when the IP owner seeks justice, the entire patent system has been rebuilt to ostracize, devalue, and eventually invalidate the infringed patent owner.

Accordingly, the Financial Accounting Standards Board (FASB), which oversees the accounting industry, should seek to evolve its accounting system to more systematically account for self-developed IP assets on financial statements. Evolving the system to more reasonably account for self-created IP assets on a balance sheet is an obvious next step that will enable IP capital financing to occur with greater ease.

Given the inherent and overt resistance to public technical

review of utilized IP assets in a product, the accounting industry needs a disruptive force to change how IP is accounted for, invested in, valued, and priced. This is where pre-revenue, IP-rich companies needing investment capital come into play. Most private equity investors overlook pre-revenue companies because the likelihood of investment recovery in the event of failure is usually zero. Pre-revenue seed companies exist in the "Startup Death Valley" where investment capital is the lifeblood needed to overcome technology adoption challenges.

Pre-revenue companies fail for many reasons, but two big factors impact them the most: lack of funding and the risk of market entry by a large incumbent with subversive pricing powers. Combined, these two limiting factors create an operating environment too hostile and repressive to coexist with large companies. However, if these early-stage companies are provided an opportunity through IP capital financing, the competition against incumbents improves remarkably.

Creating an equal playing field for businesses of all sizes is an important role for the government. Based on the failure rate of early-stage companies, the entrepreneurial system is stacked against the founder and tilted in favor of large incumbents. Said differently, government oversight of big business has been pitiful. While politicians talk about potential fixes related to antitrust, political dysfunction makes holding serial infringers accountable less likely.

AN IP PLATFORM FOR A LEVEL PLAYING FIELD

IP value exists in congruence with commercialized products. Absent commercialized products, patent value is more like an option: the right to commercialize, use, or block the use of the patented technology in the future. Non-commercialized patents are "out-of-the-money call options," meaning the patent's value is best determined based on the likely future use of the patent in a product. However, the PTAB's IPR process kills all option values by making patents unreliable.

This has enabled serial infringement of patented technology, but with the change in leadership at the USPTO in 2025, infringement will become much harder. However, the method I have described to compensate third-party IP holders should dramatically increase IP licensing. It should further give judges, expert damages witnesses, and Implementers the ability to more quickly determine patent licensing fees for use.

If transparency in a capitalist society were truthful and ethical, business leaders would support creating and enabling a fully digital patent platform that includes an FTO-to-EoU standard for understanding technology utilization. If this were to be completed, many companies may discover that a third party developed a significant portion of their technology and that paying licensing fees is the moral and ethical remedy for misuse of another's IP. Alternatively, an unethical and misleading business leader would seek to disqualify another person's IP by saying it never should have existed in the first place (a.k.a. maintaining the status quo).

Government, as the arbiter of fact and truth, should make a level playing field that balances the rights of both Inventors and Implementers. Under the AIA, however, the US patent system is wildly unbalanced in favor of Implementers. The course correction from the previous problem of patent trolls has overcompensated, and the unintended consequences have been absolutely devastating for a faction of the most creative minds in the world: the Inventor.

For Implementers, a self-declaration of an IP technology royalty rate for IP in a product changes the calculus. In general,

Implementers have been a powerful collective force that has undermined a willing licensing market for IP. Implementers should be providing a technical output that assigns FTO into technology categories of importance to the product. By doing so, and by putting additional responsibility on the Implementer to compensate third parties for their IP, the litigation and adjudication for unauthorized use becomes streamlined. Good-faith Implementers who budget for the use of third-party IP will see more reasonable judicial decisions, creating a more palatable outcome for both the Implementer and the IP holder.

Budgeting for third-party IP use for any public company worth more than $20 billion is a reasonable expectation. For corporations, categorizing their exposure to third-party patents can be determined through an FTO-to-EoU study that yields a ranking based on the good-faith willingness to operate IP space.

Proposed Independent Company (Implementer) IP Rating Framework

Company Ranking	FTO Level	EoU Level	Description
Green	90% and up	90% mapped	<ul><li>Recognizes need for in-licensing</li><li>Provides public disclosures</li><li>Open to in-licensing discussions</li><li>Limited IP litigation proceedings</li></ul>
Yellow	70% to 90%	70% mapped	<ul><li>Significant unlicensed IP being used in product(s)</li><li>Limited public disclosures</li><li>Difficult to license</li><li>Defendant in patent litigation</li></ul>
Red	50% to 70%	50% mapped	<ul><li>Outstanding IP liability to several patented inventors</li><li>Numerous open disputes or litigations</li><li>Limited transparency</li></ul>
Black	Unknown	Unknown	Unwilling market participant in the IP markets

Figure 23: An illustrative example of an IP Rating system for IP rich companies

Because the idea of an FTO public disclosure is not written in regulation or accounting guidelines, a new process can be adopted en masse on an at-will basis. As of this book's publishing, all companies fall into the "black" category of an IP compliance framework. Over time, as the IP rating system becomes commercialized, companies wanting to use IP capital as a financing means will seek a higher ranking by becoming a good-faith actor in the IP space.

Many will roll their eyes and shake their head at this suggestion, but when patent litigation defense is always "that should not have been issued in the first place," it is hard not to assume that most companies' IP departments will be reticent to adopt such a ranking system. As IPRs become less relevant, however, in-licensing at fair and reasonable rates will become more important. C-suite executives and the board of directors they serve will invariably seek to have a green IP ranking.

The process of unraveling the financial confusion of patented technology royalties begins with mapping implemented patented technology to commercialized products through an EoU study. The next step is assigning a royalty rate and then allocating the royalties to the mapped patented technology. From there, the accounting and payments are theoretically easy to figure out.

Why would this not happen? Intransigence toward third-party Inventors is the ultimate roadblock. Until then, we are left to calculate the lost licensing income for patent owners that should be paid for by Implementers. The AIA's IPR process has resulted in tens to hundreds of billions in lost licensing fees to patent owners. No wonder Implementers fight so hard to stop a marketplace for IP being created.

The great irony, of course, is that the financial exposure that the Magnificent Seven has via patent infringement is a small drop in the bucket compared to the cash these companies have on their balance sheets. In the late '90s, when patent litigation began rising in correlation with fast technological change, big companies with patent exposure started to notice. At the time, patent laws were fairly strong, and patent issuance was growing at record-breaking levels. With over 3.5 million US patents issued over the last twenty years, more patents were issued during that time than at any previous time in history. Yet pricing for patent portfolios has moved in the opposite direction relative to technology value. Instinctively, that does not make sense.

WHAT HOPE IS THERE FOR THE INVENTOR?

The individual and small business Inventor community is in dire straits. The transition from a strong to a weak patent system has devastated the morale of this important and highly regarded profession, with countless Inventors quitting their practices. While there are exceptions, most Inventors will decide to keep their inventions as trade secrets, which will eventually strain the importance of the US patent office. However, the new leadership at the USPTO is working to change that.

Regardless, trade secrets have become a growing and important asset class within IP, but believing trade secrets counterbalances the ownership of patents is a mistake. Trade secrets are not the opposite of patents, and should not be expected to fill the hole in IP protection left by the weakening of patent rights.

Despite all the proposed legislative changes to the patent system floating through Congress, none of the ideas will fix what ails patent holders. Nevertheless, the technology and ability to fix the system exist within society, but only if the regulatory capture that Big Tech has on politicians can be broken.

The ingenuity of the US patent system is still a core foundation of the US Constitution, and enabling a competent and technologically sophisticated system could invariably alter how the economy is shaped and capital allocated.

To do this, the narrative that "patents enforced through litigation are bad" must end. Moreover, Implementers using third-party patents must recognize the vital importance of Inventors, and accept that compensation for use is better than the draconian invalidation process. Recognizing the importance of patents in creating new technology should be rewarded through adoption by large incumbents, with a reasonable method of compensation to the patented IP owner.

Most importantly, the US government should recognize its role in building meaningful IP infrastructure. This would also extend to all legally protected IP assets, including copyrights and trademarks (trade secrets are another matter). The US government has woefully under-invested in the infrastructure necessary to advance invention protection. Said differently, blockchain databases are ideally built to create a patent marketplace, whereby monetization for patents used by Implementers could and should be as straightforward as a portfolio equity manager selling Company A stocks and buying Company B stocks.

The trick to make a marketplace like this work is recognizing the extraordinary role Implementers have in building a marketplace for IP. Implementers' mentality of "not invented here" is so deeply ingrained in the startup and established incumbent psyche, that the hurdle of recognizing unauthorized use of IP is misguided beyond reason.

Said differently, recognizing the problem of serial infringement of patented IP and creating an electronic mechanism to fairly compensate Inventors for use without destroying the value of an Implementer's product is tantamount to creating a fair and equitable system. In Chapter 9, I spoke about the foundational elements of patents being technical, legal, and financial, but those foundations require oversight and collaboration with a variety of regulatory agencies, as highlighted on the following chart.

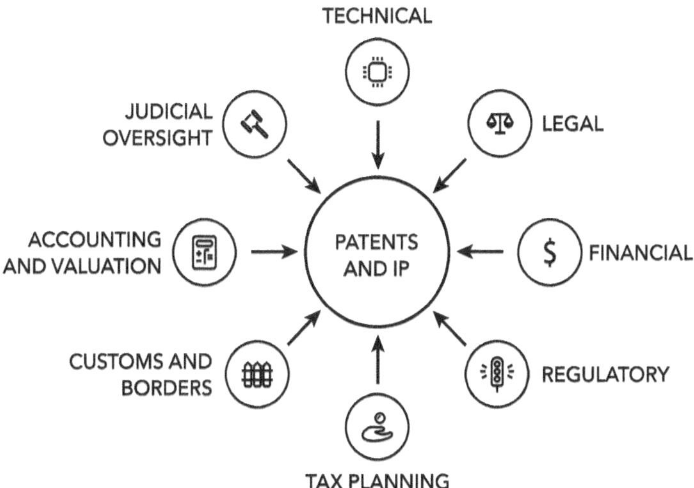

Figure 24: Patents and IP

For most patent attorneys, the broader regulatory issues related to the IP system is an unrecognized force that keeps the patent system in a conflicting stasis of misalignment. The misalignment has historically swung like a pendulum, favoring either Inventors or Implementers. The ultimate goal, however, is a form of business parity between early-stage companies and incumbents. The multitiered monetization and licensing platform I am suggesting helps the process begin to take shape. Over time, IP capital will grow into a financing option for mid-market companies, altering how investors are able to flex investments and returns.

But it cannot happen unless Implementers start believing in the IP of third parties, and recognizing that compensation for use is better than "you did not really invent that."

CHAPTER 11

REBUILD THE SYSTEM

"The AIA was supposed to be intended to have a faster, more cost effective way for an inventor to defend their patents. I should not have to be defending some of the same issues in parallel courts at the same time."

—CARRIE HAFERMEN, INVENTOR (VIA LINKEDIN POST)

BUILDING A WORKABLE SYSTEM VS. THE HARD TRUTH: SERIAL INFRINGEMENT IS NEARLY UNIVERSAL

Any flying ship aims for a soft landing, and every startup is the launch of a figurative flying machine. No engineer sets about creating a system where catastrophic failure is acceptable. However, the US economy's engineering is fundamentally built for startup companies to crash upon failure. Politicians and economists call this process "creative destruction," when the innovations of one company replace an older, outdated technology. It is a means to explain the business cycle, where failure is an acceptable outcome for a society based on competitive capitalism.

The process of creative destruction is meant to replace outdated incumbents, but the process has inverted in the last fifteen years. The startup failure rate makes it shockingly difficult to justify becoming a founder, particularly given the approximately 90 percent failure rate for pre-revenue startup companies. What is worse is that there is almost no effort to understand the failures. Literally, thousands of startup companies are never able to achieve commercial success, and their inventions often vaporize into a complete loss of capital for their founders and investors. It is a situation I have seen repeatedly throughout my career, but it is seldom, if ever, talked about or studied.

One of the greatest ironies of my career has been witnessing America's invention-protection apparatus linger behind technologically. Meanwhile technology creation and the businesses behind the technology accelerate at an exceptional pace. The entire US patent system needs to be rebuilt, and the process of categorizing inventions from application to grant needs to be revisited. It is important to recognize the value of IP creation and build a financial system around it.

Only governments can grant patents, and the current regulatory capture accrued to the large incumbents is debilitating the disruption market of Inventors. Patents are supposed to elicit the creative side of an entire population, but the AIA has slowed disruption considerably in the last fifteen years, resulting in value accruing to a concentrated number of companies, particularly the Magnificent Seven.

If done correctly, an IP system should enable the adoption of technology through a nation's economy to ensure the highest and best technology is used in products and services. Adopting the best technology is often easier and more efficient to implement than trying to figure out patent work-arounds that often keep internal R&D teams spinning their wheels. Moreover, in-house engineers and product design specialists can become more efficient by reviewing, analyzing, and recognizing that certain patents already resolved a technical difficulty in the best way that enables a product created by an Implementer. C-suites and R&D departments would be much wiser to in-license the patented technology instead of trying to design around it. Unfortunately, C-suite leadership would rather send a team of engineers to figure out a "work-around" of the better-patented technology. Oftentimes, the work-around will still infringe on someone else's patent. And worse, the work-around incorporated into the product makes it less useful than the original patented technology that could have been in-licensed.

As a result, the corresponding compensation for using another's IP nearly always requires litigation, or the implicit expectation of litigation if an agreement is not reached. The notion of an efficient and transparent patent licensing process is completely antithetical to how the marketplace is currently structured. Instead, the efficiencies gained by Implementers are through infringement, followed by invalidation. Accordingly, litigation is the best and primary way for patent holders to license alleged infringers, which acts as a trip wire for the alleged infringer to petition for an IPR.

Patent litigation is deliberately slow, and the AIA added numerous extra steps that slow the process even further, despite its claims it would be faster and more efficient when first enacted. In an operating environment of move fast and break things, patents move glacially slow. Alleged infringers move slower, and with only a twenty-year patent life, justice delayed is justice denied.

The rampant political interference in the US patent system has been a red herring. Legislatures have been told that the patent system delays innovation, but they have never been presented with a proposal that creates a level playing field.

A fundamentally fair system would incentivize collaboration, transparently recognize the utilization of IP in commercialized products, and provide reasonable compensation for the use of the IP. This utopian idea of fair payment for the use of IP requires the development of technical accounting for utilized IP within products or services. Right now, the process is arcane and fundamentally lacking a mechanized system of accounting, valuation, pricing, and fair trade.

Creating a robust public-private-run platform for IP and patent monetization, investment, and licensing using blockchain can transform how IP assets are tracked, valued, priced, licensed, and utilized. Further, a digital patent platform that uses blockchain can incorporate an Implementer's royalty bases electronically. By recognizing that the IP and patent system needs to know the royalty base of commercialized products, a modernized digital IP system becomes feasible. More importantly, the digital tracking system for understanding the technology used in a product enables an IP marketplace and investment center. The enabling factor to make it happen is not possible unless the government is willing to build it. Once it exists, holding Implementers to account for the IP technology it adopts in its products will become the foundation for an IP marketplace.

Governments can rebuild the wall of IP protection for patents. We have the technology. Building it is not the issue; rather, do we have the will to create it?

No Inventor applying for a patent wants to have two separate validation processes enacted on their patent; however, the PTAB's IPR does just that, and the uncertainty of the IPR process has cast a pall on the entire US patent system. The implicit impact is that patents are only useful to large companies, and the long-term impact is the loss of individual Inventors who are quitting the system. No longer is the patent system equipped to protect individual and small company Inventors from the prying eyes and enacting Implementers of large incumbents.

The current muddled process does not need to exist this way. Financial liquidity tied to patented technology adopted into products is the best path forward. Investment in innovative, early-stage companies does not have to go to the best "pitch deck" creator. Instead, a robust IP system can enable the best technology to be adopted by all entrepreneurs and companies in a sophisticated, smart way. By making patent and IP licensing easier, the adoption of the best technology in products, not the cheapest work-around, becomes the standard for product development.

Technology exists to understand, account, track, and allocate income from a product being sold to the underpinning technology that enables it. Like a condominium building that has 350 units that are separately owned, a commercialized product should be able to track the adopted technology that enables the product to work. Identifying, classifying, and estimating the IP value created from the product's sale is the panacea for the serial infringement that currently exists within the marketplace. But it is not easy.

In the context of media, such as television, movies, music, or entertainment, creators are highly cognizant of using other people's IP, such as trademarks or copyrights. For even the smallest use of another person's IP, creators are aware of the need for compensation for use. In 2025, when the Kansas City Chiefs went to the Super Bowl to attempt to win their third title in three straight years, IP strategists highlighted the potential earning capacity that Pat Riley, head coach of the Los Angeles Lakers in the 1980s and 1990s, stood to earn for his trademark of "Three-Peat."

Recognizing use of another person's IP is intuitive common sense for some types of IP, but for patents, it is a different story. Pat Riley heard one of his players mention "Three-Peat" shortly before the Lakers won their third title in 1988 and sent his IP attorney to take ownership of the term. Since then, Pat Riley has earned an unknown amount of royalties every time a team wins three championships in a row.

Without ignoring the effort required to win three championships, but also recognizing the limited effort in creating the term "Three-Peat," an understanding and illustration of the difference between the efforts of a patented Inventor and a trademark holder should highlight why patent IPRs are such an intolerably cruel process.

Inventors who apply for patents and have them granted go through an extraordinarily hard process to get a patent. Compensation for unauthorized use should be recognized and paid for with as quick of a response as someone who wants to use the term "Three-Peat." However, it is not that way for patent owners in the current system. Since recognizing infringement for a patent is much harder than trademarks or copyrights, a digital platform that enables identification of use with a quick means for compensation for use of another person's patented IP is the necessary bridge for fixing the problems that ail the US patent system.

THE ECONOMICS OF LIQUIDITY IN IP AND THE MISNOMERS OF PATENT TROLLS

An Implementer transacting patent licenses freely in the patent space is a grand idea built on good-faith licensing. Creating a digitized system that enables an Implementer's FTO through a blockchain system where compensation for use is enabled through smart contracts creates a simple path of licensing alignment. A digital system that functions as a multilevel monetization platform, providing legitimate FTO for Implementers, will undoubtedly be beneficial to patent holders seeking compensation for the use of their patents.

Equally important would be the platform's financing options for early-stage companies with patents. Private investors seeking early-stage opportunities can search, contact, and directly interact with Inventors using a fully digital platform.

A USPTO blockchain system could dramatically alter the agency's scope and oversight. The "tentacles" of economic activity that could flow through a blockchain system to companies of all sizes would be transformative. Since patents are a constitutional right, a government-enabled system designed to enable prosecution, issuance, investment, and licensing of patented technology in a transparent, frictionless, and scalable system is well within the federal government's rights. The immutable ledger of patent information can be housed in a singular system that could generate incredible returns over the medium to long term.

Of course, no one is obligated to license or buy a patent, but if the patent owner believes there is infringement, the patent owner has the right to enforce its rights through the court system. This is the implicit understanding of patent ownership that has endured since the US adopted its patent law in 1790.

Elon Musk famously said, "Patents are for the weak." Unfortunately, that is only true if the patent system is built as a weak system. In a well-regulated and developed patent system, patents make the world every company's R&D center. It opens the world to invention and innovation that is often outside the scope of research for some companies or research labs. Patents, if viewed through the appropriate lens, open innovation beyond the confines of corporate campuses. Patents allow the Inventor in his garage or small office to compete on a more balanced level with the large companies. At least, it used to be that way until the AIA. The AIA has weakened patents to the point of a participation award at best, or more likely, a ticket to patent litigation. Patent litigation is a nightmare ride of gaslighting and traumatic disputes over technical nuance that can end with the patent holder losing more than everything. It does not have to be that way. Patents can still carry value, but the pricing and valuation mechanisms are all off, and the system needs to be fixed and realigned to match the incentives for all stakeholders.

In the place where IP and finance intersect, a granted patent is an option to use the technology. It comes with a financial cost that is unknown to potential Implementers because pricing of patented technology is not disclosed, or is hidden, or is unstated. The patent should afford the owner the right to use, prevent use, or license use, but the current process is woefully inefficient.

There is also the right to sell or sublicense, which are completely acceptable forms of business, but over the last two decades, patent licensing has become synonymous with patent trolls. However, patent trolls were not the evil we were made to believe. The patent trolls were acting as financial arbitrageurs to profit from the opportunity. Not recognizing the recovery value that patent trolls offer failed startups, the AIA overcorrected in its efforts to prevent excess patent litigation. Unfortunately, the cure has been worse than the disease, and despite the false narrative, patents are not the problem.

In reality, Implementers rampantly infringing on third-party patented technology are the issue. "Efficient infringement" is a term that has caught on because it is happening with regularity. Most industries have a wolf pack mentality, whereby the biggest tech companies are the alpha leaders, and all those in the wolf pack follow their lead. Unfortunately, the Big Tech companies have a radical notion that everything they develop and produce has been invented by their own team of engineers, which is not true.

Regardless, Big Tech's cognitive dissonance about using third-party patents means any third-party patent owner requesting a patent license for use must be denied. In fact, ask Big Tech for a patent licensing, and eventually the patent owner will be called a patent troll. Because Big Tech carries these views, it permeates through all the industries the Magnificent Seven lead.

The anti-patent views of Big Tech trickles down through industry and has created an ethos of anti-patent sentiment. Undoing the current stasis that embattles the patent system is feasible, but only if there is a willingness to do so. The incentive lies in creating liquidity, investment opportunities, and capitalist principles. American Inventors, however, are resilient, creative, and ingenious and are working hard to strengthen the patent system.

THE FINANCIALIZATION OF IP

Private credit lending has grown into a $2 trillion business by 2023, a ten-time increase over the previous fifteen years. A competitor to traditional bank lending, private credit loans have interest rates more favorable to the lender because the risk is higher. Typical private lending participants include private equity, family offices, or hedge funds, but in recent years, it has expanded beyond that to larger institutions.

Regardless of the lender, asset collateral is needed to support the debt facility, and the assets that support these investments are reflected on the balance sheet. All lenders' first and primary concern when issuing a loan is how the company plans to pay back the debt. Based on the borrower's risk profile, a credit rating is established, and the riskier a borrower, the higher the interest rate.

While every investor hopes its early-stage investments become unicorns, the reality suggests that most will fail. If private debt markets are expected to flourish, they will need a better mechanism for recovering lost investment through asset recovery. A digitized patent system becomes the base platform to enable investment recovery, depending on the situation. If there is a transparent understanding of IP value that is fundamentally tied to cash flow, recovery values will improve dramatically.

For most private credit lenders, the loan-to-value (LTV) ratios for IP are much lower than tangible assets. However, if the patent system becomes more reliable, a lender can expect LTV ratios for intangible assets to improve, as highlighted in the following table:

Debt Collateral Assets	Loan-to-Value Collateral in 2025	LTV Collateral with Blockchain IP in 2030+
Working Capital	90% to 95%	90% to 95%
Property, Plant, and Equipment	50% to 75%	50% to 75%
Developed Technology	5% to 25%	50% to 90%
Brands and Trademarks	5% to 25%	90% to 95%
Any Other Intangible Asset	Unlikely to Be Used	10% to 25%

Figure 25: Loan-to-Value Ratios

While debt lenders will take a security interest lien on legally protected hard IP assets (i.e., patents, trademarks, etc.), the uncertainty makes them ill-suited to serve as collateral for debt lending. Recovering IP assets, particularly patents, in bankruptcy is too hard after the legislative changes from the AIA.

In fact, for debt lenders to include IP assets as collateral, they prefer to see a steady stream of cash flows driven by the IP, which the platform I am suggesting allows for.

For most companies, however, internal IP management is typically concerned with creation of IP, and less concerned with the active financial management of its developed IP. Financial management of IP concerns the potential income or capital opportunities that could be generated through IP. Most people are well aware of the licensing income available to IP owners of all types, but the concept of IP capital is less developed.

IP debt lending that aligns fundamentally with the survival of IP assets in the event of bankruptcy is a critically missing component enabling IP debt as an investment security. Too often, I have seen bankrupt companies with soft IP or grey IP that cannot be monetized in the recovery of investment from the bankrupt companies. However, with a digitized patent system, a company's ability to monetize IP that is already being used in the marketplace becomes easier. Moreover, private enterprise that enables the active management of IP and patents becomes a streamlined internal process. By creating a system that allows for the active management and oversight of patents and IP, a new market for IP becomes feasible, but it requires the administrative power of a country's government to build the system that will enable it.

CHAPTER 12

BUILDING AND PAYING FOR THE NEW PATENT SYSTEM

"The nation badly needs new highways. The good of our people, of our economy, and of our defense, requires that construction of these highways be undertaken at once."

—PRESIDENT DWIGHT EISENHOWER,
WRITTEN TO CONGRESS IN 1955

BUILDING THE SYSTEM

As America's government goes through a complete overhaul under the new presidential administration, the US patent system's revamp as a new-era platform is poised to be part of that (r)evolution. Like an old, dodgy sports stadium that is past its time, the new US patent system needs to be built from the ground up, right alongside the old one. Keep the parts that were working fairly well. Include a few of the old traditions that made the old system timeless. Then, let the old system continue to operate as it always has until it is time to wind it down.

Of course, the transition from old system to new system will need to happen gradually. Once the system is ready, it undoubtedly will have kinks to be worked out, but once it is live, the Inventor class applying for patents will be given a choice between the old system and the new system for how they would prefer to have their patent prosecuted. That choice between the two systems will act as a self-governing measure for a gradual transition.

Most likely, individuals and small businesses will be quick to adopt the new system, but I can anticipate old stodgy companies will prefer the grey area of technology attribution in which they currently exist. C-suites and the boards they report to may be reticent to transition their patent prosecution to a system that offers more transparency and disclosure than they are historically used to, and honestly, that is fine. Large entities' slow transition to patent prosecution on the new system will allow government operators to work out the kinks and streamline the process.

New features and options can be added to the system based on the administrator's timeline. The early adopters of the new system will feel the economic benefits quickly, and a wave of economic change for Inventors will enable many startups to escape the Startup Death Valley. After all, capital is the water and lifeblood of an early-stage company. Providing capital to inventive entrepreneurs will enable growth from the ground up.

The new system can create a more holistic approach to government support of early-stage companies. Small Business Administration (SBA), grants, loans, private investment, and community support can surround new startups as they build new businesses with the confidence that the patented IP they are creating is secured and valid. Remove the uncertainty of IPR invalidation, and the system's predictability will enable mainstream institutional investment (i.e., pensions, insurance, mutual funds, etc.). By first building the system with seed-level companies, inevitably, more mature companies will utilize IP capital investment to fund future operations. Eventually, IP debt with a security interest lien will enable patented technology to be recycled and reused in a much more efficient and meaningful way.

In a reformed patent system, a failed startup's patented IP will live and exist outside of the failed company for future enablement and use instead of being killed by the draconian IPR process that exists in the AIA. In the unfortunate case of a startup's failure, which is more likely to occur than not, the patented technology will live on to earn a recovery for its investor. Recovery of lost investment is a critical part of investing that many VCs seem unwilling to examine as a failure of their overall investment thesis. It does not have to be that way for VC investors.

In a new blockchain patent system, patent and IP monetization will enable several financing methods that had previously not been used. The multilateral uses of IP financing through a digitized system will forever transform how IP capital, monetization, licensing, and strategy are conducted. Moreover, patent- and IP-focused startups will provide their investors legitimate risk management that will prevent IP theft or misuse. By digitizing the IP system, the financial opportunities will leapfrog every other system currently in existence.

Of course, I hope that the US government will build a new blockchain-based patent system that incorporates the financial aspects of a patent into a robust system. By digitizing and making transparent the types of technology being granted by the USPTO, Implementers will be able to pay reasonable licensing fees through an easy, honest, and ethical system that is stored on a public ledger. The policy of "destroy the Inventor's patented IP from ever existing" will no longer be the policy of USPTO.

Never before has there been a quick, simple, and transparent means of paying licensing fees. The old system was an analog one that favored information asymmetry. The information asymmetry distorted the market in favor of companies worth over $20 billion in market capitalization, but the new system will level the playing field while creating liquidity and a secondary market for trading IP-backed investment securities. Once CFOs, CEOs, and their C-suites adjust to the new reality, IP financing will move upstream from startups to mid-market companies. The transformation to company balance sheets will be extraordinary, and GAAP principles will evolve to account for intangible assets, specifically Developed Technology, in a more systematic and uniform manner.

While the systematic transfer and convergence of debt and equity financial markets into a government-backed IP financing market seems far-fetched, the opportunity to realize it is more possible now than it ever has been. This is not a field of dreams, however. Build it wrong and it is a colossal waste of money. Moreover, paying for it will need congressional approval and a sign-off by the president. Considering how deeply Big Tech is entrenched in the pockets of politicians, is agreement ever possible? And if by some miracle, they did agree, how would the system be paid for?

PAYING FOR A NEW SYSTEM

The federal government is notoriously bad at commercializing ideas into programs. Despite the best intent, rollouts are often lackluster. There are lots of reasons for this, but I would hazard that the lack of profit motive limits the appropriate investment in creating a meaningful system. By recognizing the vast profit-making potential of creating a financialized patent and IP system, the simple path is following the Highway Revenue Act (HRA) of 1956, which created a trust fund to build a nationwide road system.

In reality, the HRA of '56 was a bond issuance that was paid for by a tax fee per gallon of gasoline sold, which paid back the bonds held in the trust. To pay the bonds back, the HRA shifted how the federal government collected fees from "a license to make" to "a license to use," allowing the start of a federal gasoline tax. A tax that lives on today and funds the continued maintenance of the finest highway system in the world. A highway system that enables the transport of commerce across the entire country.

Similarly, updating the US patent system to be brought into the twenty-first century through a patent trust fund backed by the faith of the US government's Department of the Treasury could be used to build an ideal blockchain system, particularly by hiring the best blockchain software engineers in the world. Pay them market rates with exceptional bonuses when certain milestones are hit, and ensure that the system rolls out flawlessly by first building it for startups and pre-revenue companies that are seeking IP protection and investment IP capital financing.

By investing directly in seed funding situations with patents, the initial price setting for patented technology within a product is a genuine means to establish a royalty rate. From those early instances, pricing and valuation mechanics can exist in congruence. Then, as the product evolves over time, and new versions of the product are created, the Implementer can appropriately readjust its determined royalty rates to reflect the technology and IP's origin. The ongoing requests for IP licensing will continue, but with an appropriately determined IP licensing budget, Implementers can compensate where appropriate, and free market negotiations will help reallocate the royalty price paid for third-party technology. By building a marketplace with consistent terms, market forces will begin to appropriately value IP because there will be an actual market for transaction pricing.

The fees generated by administering a patent system on a blockchain that is financialized and liquid will generate vast sums of wealth that are broadly distributed. Such a platform will wield enormous power to pay the patent trust fund back quickly. Fees that will quickly be reinvested in the other legalized pillars of IP, and (eventually) in paying down the national debt.

If the USPTO's economist estimates that patents support a $7.8 trillion economy, then providing IP capital to seed companies at 0.5 percent of that patent economy would equate to $39 billion to be invested into startups with patents. That kind of capital moves mountains for seed-level companies. Combine a small amount of public capital with private capital, and seed-level companies will likely flourish rather than fail nearly 90 percent of the time. But that is a long way off.

WHAT ABOUT CURRENT PATENT HOLDERS ON THE OLD SYSTEM?

The circumstantial evidence of an unspoken conspiracy to objectively weaken patent rights to the benefit of Big Tech is simply overwhelming. From the patent litigation and IPR statistics, to the deep lobbying dollars that influenced the passage of the AIA, to the broad data showing Big Tech is serially infringing patented technology, the outcomes to weaken patents has had an outsized positive impact for Big Tech. However, Big Tech has gotten too greedy, and the recent presidential administrative change opens the door for a massive change to the US patent system.

Given how slanted the playing field has been in favor of Big Tech since the AIA became law, the financial exposure has grown too large over the last eight years. For far too long, Big Tech has concealed its patent infringement with the worst defense of all time: that patents should not have been issued in the first place.

Oh, the trauma I have witnessed of Inventors who have lost their patents in such a cruel, callous, and heartless manner. The various means of invalidating patents in the US have been astonishingly awful to witness. Inventors, whoever they are, wherever they are, are one of the most treasured professions in the history of humankind. What they have gone through since the IPR was enacted in 2013 has been brutal. Even worse has been the pompous and indifferent attitudes toward individual and small business patent owners that permeate Big Tech IP departments. It elicits a strong desire to organize a class-action lawsuit on behalf of all patent holders against the biggest lobbying companies for the AIA, which undoubtedly would include five of the Magnificent Seven.

Add in the DOJ's antitrust victories against Google and its ongoing litigations with Amazon, Apple, and others, and antitrust settlement payments into the patent trust fund from the AIA's biggest beneficiaries seems reasonable. Included in the settlement should be refunds and restitution to all patent holders who have lost their patents through the IPR process. The IPR's invalidation rates have been way too high, and the lack of a time-bound review process is flatly unreasonable. Too many Inventors are losing their patents in their sixth year or later of granted patent ownership. No other country has an invalidation process that is allowed to invalidate that far after the fact. Six months to a year after a patent's issuance seems like the appropriate window to challenge validity by the public after the USPTO issues a patent. After that, tough luck invalidating an issued patent. The patent stays until it expires. If you infringe, stop using it or pay for it or face adjudication.

Fortunately, the first nine months of 2025 saw significant reforms come to the patent office. Starting with the former interim director's decision to use discretionary denials of IPR while promoting the use of post-grant review procedures to test the validity of a granted patent after its issuance. The meaningful changes Deputy Director Coke Morgan Stewart has enacted during her tenure has elicited more hope and excitement for the inventive community than at any other time in the last fifteen years. Combined with Director John Squires's "Born Strong" patent initiative, the patent system is having a reckoning that will have significant repercussions across the economy.

But the days of callously taking away Inventors' patents needs to become a rarity, which only happens in the most egregious cases of patent mis-prosecution errors. With a new digitized patent system, making a payment for use will become easy, predictable, and built into an Implementer's budget from the beginning of each year. Self-declaration (in private or public) of a Developed Technology royalty rate enables friendly licensing with a gating range of potential licensing rates. In-licensing another person's patent would take no longer than a few weeks of negotiation and rate setting, resulting in a satisfactory agreement between licensor and licensee. No longer will Inventors have to live in fear of invalidation after a certain point after the initial USPTO examination and secondary public validation gauntlet.

On the other hand, Implementers can utilize the patent and IP system to make payment for in-licensed IP and patents, providing real and legitimate FTO. The IP value allocation example I created is an Implementer-friendly financial design for assigning value to technology into three primary categories: patents, trade secrets, and know-how. The delineation of value ascribed to each component of Developed Technology is an evolution of a US GAAP that should be adopted if IP capital becomes a legitimate financial arrangement that becomes widespread. As adoption of IP capital financing by Implementers moves up the value chain to medium and large companies, previous estimates of IP value allocation will become benchmarking indications of pricing, which is the virtuous cycle of value creation. The evolution of IP finance will change as IP debt and IP equity start creating new financial measures to support the percent allocations to the assigned technology value.

Potential Ranges of Technology Royalty Rate Allocation

Patent and Technology Owner	Selected RR Weighting	Range of Weighting	Negotiated Royalty Weightings
Apple Patents	5%	5% to 20%	Most valuable patents contributing
Third Parties	3%	1% to 10%	Cross-licensing value that is highly debatable and could result in litigation
Off-Patent/Expired/ Indemnified	0%	0%	Limited to no controversy
Unlicensed Patent Liabilities	2%	1% to 5%	Least valued technology contribution to a product, per implementers
Apple Trade Secrets	90% combined	55% to 90%	Current implementer belief on Technology IP value to a product
Apple Know-How			
TOTAL	10%	100%	

Figure 26: Illustrative example of technology royalty rate allocation

A royalty rate weighting calculation is an Implementer decision that can change based on market feedback, subject matter expertise, and reasonable apportionment considerations of a technology IP or patent to the product. The court system that has enabled patent litigation will always be necessary to resolve disputes, but if Implementers conduct apportionment of technology IP and patents as I am describing, the courts will be able to more quickly and accurately adjudicate IP disputes. More importantly, however, are the royalty rate guardrails that are determined by the Implementer that will enable better negotiating positions for licensee and licensor. If the system is built correctly, good-faith monetization efforts will create an exceptional economic output that will be spread throughout the economy, rather than having it concentrated in the hands of a few gigantic companies. All that is required is a reasonable framework that can adjust to the facts and circumstances specific to the product and associated IP, creating a means to reasonably determine IP value attribution to a product.

THE TECHNOLOGY, IP, AND PATENT SYSTEM FRAMEWORK

The combination of ideas presented throughout this book are not unique or novel, but rather they represent the convergence of ideas across patents, finance, accounting, investing, and regulatory oversight. By taking these core concepts and functions, and overlaying them into a new system, a new economic platform that grows in congruence with technology development across all types of innovation is possible.

If the patent system I am describing for monetizing patents is created, it can expand beyond patents to all forms of legally protected IP. If done correctly, the financialization of legally protected IP has the capacity to transform the economy by systematically creating a more harmonized and equitable capital allocation for creators, Inventors, artists, scientists, and researchers. At the center of that IP platform would be a government acting in the best interest of its people, rather than the corporations that lobby the government.

The Developed Technology intangible asset valuation construct explained throughout this book is the blueprint for all countries and companies to account for, value, and price the intangible technology assets developed. It is a multifaceted system that places creators at the center of inspirational ideations. More importantly, it enables freedom to operate without the hostile act of invalidating someone else's hard work.

A digital IP system creates a garden for IP to grow, share, and collaborate with, instead of IP for cutting, fighting, and slashing. Of course, patents and IP assets will always be a double-edged sword with the capacity to injure if not wielded correctly, but the digitization of patented IP onto a government platform provides a safe operating environment for business to be conducted in peaceful negotiations. These negotiations can then be discreetly disclosed through the IP system in a way that enables IP pricing and value benchmarking. With financial benchmarking of IP licensing and sale on a legitimate IP platform, using IP to avoid taxes will forever be transformed, and the OECD will have to rethink its tax treaties to ensure that each country is accurately receiving its due tax payments.

At a certain point after the creation of the new patent system, the ongoing administrative fees will not only pay back the bonds in the patent trust fund but will also start adding an inexhaustible amount of income to it—fees that can be used to pay down the debt or finance federal programs for Social Security, healthcare, or solving homelessness. The power of liquid IP investments, assets, and monetization will have a massive multiplier effect on the economy. It is a study that government agencies across the globe should be working to determine, in collaboration with each other.

After all, the WIPO recently celebrated intangible asset values at corporations reaching $80 trillion! As of this book's publication, intangible asset value is an illiquid asset that sits relatively frozen on corporate balance sheets. The multiplier impact of creating liquidity in IP, a small portion of intangible assets, will drive economic growth that the US and OECD economists should measure. Patents are only a small portion of that total, and yet the creation of financial liquidity from the US patent system will create countless jobs in a multiplier effect. From the investment program in early-stage startup companies to the financial administration of licensing programs to the distribution of licensing fees paid rather than buried in litigation, the economic ramifications will have a meaningful impact on the entire global economy. The reallocation of capital diffused through the variety of monetization and business opportunities created by blockchain patent systems is nearly inexhaustible.

The fundamental creation, administration, and evolution of the blockchain patent system creates economic and business opportunities in a systematically sustainable, yet creatively destructive manner. It is a system that enables a business cycle that recognizes the multitiered reality of the IP system, and deals with company restructuring more systematically. The USPTO has a mission "to drive US innovation, inclusive capitalism, and global competitiveness." A digital IP system on the blockchain is the best path forward for that mission to be achieved.

ACKNOWLEDGMENTS

I could not have made it for twenty-six years in the IP industry without a lot of help from people along the way. Learning and understanding the trade craft of IP valuation and finance has not been an easy road, but there have been an incredible number of people who have helped me through the journey. Without their guidance, support, tutelage, and affirmation throughout the years, this book would not have been possible. Somewhere along the way, you were there for me, and I am forever grateful for you:

Roy D'Souza, Ryan Carter, John Seidensticker, Tom Hotchstatter, Aaron Mollin, Art Nutter, John Miret, Ryan Dunigan, Jeremy Fallt, James Tolson, Steve O'Doriso, Michael Jenet, Shayna Truillo, Josh Gammon, Kirk Anderson, Jeff Schell, Alex Martin, Jill Carey, Ocean Tomo, PwC, R. Matthew Clark, Timothy O'Connor, Brent Maier, Adam Ortega, Brian Leahy, Robert Rath, Jozef Kavuliak, Garry Stone, Rosanna Gandiaga, Sylvia White, Krishnan Chandrasekhar, James Malacowski, Ed Fish, Mitch Rosenfeld, Ian McClure, Trevor Blum, Dan McEldowney, Bakir Ibresivic, Haris Hadziabdic, Brent Reynolds, Liz Quinlavin, Nash and Mia Ream, Chad Morrissey, Colin Ryan,

Brandon de la Houssaye, Darius Sankey, Timothy Binney, Sean Sheridan, Tom Ryan, Ron Freisleben, Gervais "Mama Bear" Wright, Justin Liddell, Mark Paterson, Amy Ellis, John Amster, EC DeSpain, Julie Burke, Merritt Fletcher, Carrie Hafeman, Warren Tuttle, Doug Pittman, Angus Bower, Mark Meijer, Lane 8, and Aimee Taublieb.

GLOSSARY

TERM	DEFINITION
AIA	The America Invents Act (AIA) of 2011 significantly reformed US patent law, most notably shifting it from a "first-to-invent" system to a "first-inventor-to-file" system, aligning the US with most other countries and emphasizing the first person to file for a patent, not necessarily the first to invent it. Key changes include establishing post-grant challenges (like Inter Partes Review), creating a one-year grace period for Inventors to file after disclosing their work, and reducing fees for solo Inventors and startups.
Alice	Shorthand for the SCOTUS ruling in *Alice Corp. v. CLS Bank International*, a landmark 2014 Supreme Court case that established a two-part test for determining patent eligibility, especially for software, holding that abstract ideas implemented on generic computers are not patentable.
APA	Advanced Pricing Arrangement is a term used in international tax treaties with MNEs to ensure all participating countries where the MNE operates pay their fair share of taxes to the taxing authorities of a country.
API	Application Programming Interface is a set of rules and protocols that allow different software programs to communicate and exchange data with each other.
AR	Augmented Reality

TERM	DEFINITION
ARR	Annualized Recurring Revenue is the predictable, normalized yearly income from subscriptions and recurring contracts, crucial for SaaS and subscription businesses to forecast growth, measure financial health, and assess long-term value by focusing on consistent revenue streams, not one-time sales. It is calculated by annualizing monthly recurring revenue (MRR) or adding annual contracts and expansion revenue, and subtracting churn and contraction.
AST	Allied Security Trust
AUM	Assets Under Management
AVP	Apple Vision Pro
Big Four	The four largest public accounting firms: Deloitte, KPMG, EY, PwC.
BRI	Broadest Reasonable Interpretation is a standard used by the USPTO, especially in patent reviews, to interpret claim terms with their "plain meaning" as understood by a skilled person, but within the context of the patent's own written description, allowing for the widest possible scope that is still supported and not contradicted by the specification.
CEO	Chief Executive Officer
CFO	Chief Financial Officer
Claim Chart (or EoU)	A detailed, often tabular, document that visually maps the specific elements (limitations) of a patent claim against features of an accused product, process, or prior art to determine if infringement or invalidity exists, also called an EoU.
Cloud Computing or Cloud	The practice of using a network of remote servers hosted on the internet to store, manage, and process data, rather than a local server or a personal computer.
CVC	Corporate Venture Capital is when large established companies invest their own funds directly into external startups, primarily for strategic reasons like accessing new tech, markets, or talent, alongside potential financial returns, acting as a bridge between traditional VC and corporate development to foster innovation and future growth.
Developed Technology	New or improved tools, systems, methods, and processes created from scientific knowledge to solve problems, enhance capabilities, boost efficiency, and improve quality of life, moving beyond basic concepts to practical, often modernized applications like smartphones or advanced robotics. It signifies an advancement, offering better solutions than existing technology, and can involve complex innovations from research and development (R&D) to commercialization and market adoption.

TERM	DEFINITION
DTSA	Defense of Trade Secrets Act
EFF	Electronic Frontier Foundation
EoU (or Claim Chart)	Evidence of Use: An analysis of patent claims compared to the technical specifications of a product or service that is indicative of utilization of the patent. EoUs are often used to convince Implementers, litigators, and/or judges that a patent is being infringed, also called a Claim Chart.
EPS	Earnings per Share is a key financial metric showing how much profit a company generates for each outstanding share of its stock, calculated by dividing net income (minus preferred dividends) by the number of common shares, indicating profitability and value for investors, and used in ratios like the Price-to-Earnings (P/E) ratio.
FASB	Financial Accounting Standards Board
FIL/BIL	Father-in-Law/Brother-in-Law
FTO	Freedom to Operate: An analysis of a product that helps determine the number of patented technologies that exist within a product or service.
GAAP	Generally Accepted Accounting Procedures
GDP	Gross Domestic Product
IFRS	International Financial Reporting Standards
IP	Intellectual Property
IPR	Inter Partes Review
LOT Network	License on Transfer Network
M&A	Mergers and Acquisitions
Magnificent Seven	The seven dominant, mega-cap US technology stocks—Apple, Microsoft, Amazon, Alphabet (Google), Nvidia, Meta Platforms (Facebook), and Tesla—that have a market capitalization above 1 trillion USD.
MNE	Multinational Enterprise is a company that owns or controls production, services, or assets in at least two countries, with headquarters in a "home" country and operations in "host" countries, leveraging resources globally for strategic vision, market access, and efficiency, rather than just exporting goods.

TERM	DEFINITION
MVP	Minimum Viable Product is the simplest version of a new product with just enough core features to be usable, attract early adopters, and gather validated learning about customer needs with minimal effort and cost, allowing businesses to test their core hypothesis before full investment.
NFC	Near Field Communications
NIL	Name, Image, Likeness
NSA	National Security Agency
OECD	Organisation for Economic Co-operation and Development
Patent Hold Out	Patent "Hold Out" is the practice of companies routinely ignoring patents and resisting patent owner demands because the odds of getting caught are small.
Patent Hold Up	Patent "Hold Up" occurs when a patent owner sues a company when it is most vulnerable—after it has implemented a technology—and is able to win a settlement because it is too late for the company to change course.
Patent Stack	The total number of patents that are being used by a product or service.
Patent Trolls (a.k.a. PAEs or NPEs)	A derogatory name for a company or group that obtains the rights to one or more patents to profit by means of licensing or litigation, rather than by producing its own goods or services. Also called a Patent Assertion Entity (less pejorative), or a Non-Practicing Entity. The interchangeable terms are often conflated, and end up including entities such as Universities, Research Labs, or Invention Institutions.
PCAOB	Public Company Accounting Oversight Board
PE	Private Equity
PGR	Post-Grant Review
PoC	Proof of Concept is evidence, typically derived from an experiment or pilot project, which demonstrates that a design concept, business proposal, etc., is feasible.
Preponderance of Evidence Standard	The "Preponderance of Evidence" standard uses the analogy of a scale: It means tipping the scale slightly in one's favor, showing the claim is more likely true than not (over 50 percent probability) and is the standard used in most civil cases, unlike the stricter "beyond a reasonable doubt" in criminal cases.

TERM	DEFINITION
PTAB	Patent Trial and Appeal Board
QR Code	Quick Response Code
R&D	Research and Development
RFID	Radio Frequency Identification
ROI	Return on Investment
Royalty Rate	The percentage or fixed amount paid by a user (licensee) to an owner (licensor) for using their asset, like a patent, trademark, music, or natural resource, as defined in a licensing agreement.
Royalty Stack	The cumulative cost of multiple patents that a single product or service uses and must license to avoid infringement, including owned or third-party patents.
RPX	Rational Patent Exchange
Rule 11	Federal Rule of Civil Procedure 11 (FRCP 11), which requires that all legal documents be signed by an attorney or unrepresented party and certifies that the content is not for an improper purpose and is supported by law and evidence.
SaaS	Software as a Service
SCOTUS	Supreme Court of the United States
SDK	Software Development Kit is a set of tools for third-party developers to use in producing applications using a particular framework or platform.
SEP	Standard Essential Patents (SEPs) protect inventions critical for implementing industry-wide technical standards, like Wi-Fi, 5G, or USB, ensuring products from different companies can work together (interoperability); patent holders agree to license these patents on Fair, Reasonable, and Non-Discriminatory (FRAND) terms to foster innovation, but disputes often arise over licensing fees, making them a major focus in technology law and policy.
SOX	The Sarbanes-Oxley Act (SOX) of 2002 is a US federal law that established stricter financial reporting and corporate governance rules for public companies, aiming to restore investor confidence after major accounting scandals (like Enron and WorldCom) by increasing accountability, accuracy, and transparency in financial disclosures and audits, making executives personally responsible for financial statements.
STEM	Science, Technology, Engineering, and Math

TERM	DEFINITION
Technology Stack	The total amount of identifiable technology in a product or service that includes patents, trade secrets, or other critical technology.
UCC	Uniform Commercial Code is a comprehensive set of laws governing commercial transactions in the US, covering everything from sales and leases to banking and secured loans, aiming to standardize business rules across states, though specific filing codes (like Article 9 filings) create public records for secured debts.
USPTO	United States Patent and Trademark Office
VC	Venture Capital is funding provided to early-stage, high-growth potential startups and small businesses in exchange for equity (ownership).

REFERENCES

The reference list is broken up by chapter and alphabetized within each section to aid readers in finding further material relevant to the content of each chapter.

CHAPTER 1: HOW FINANCE EXPLAINS THE BROKEN US PATENT SYSTEM

Behrens, David. "The Tabarrok Curve: A Call for Patent Reform in the US." The Economics Review, accessed January 19, 2026. https://theeconreview. com/2018/03/13/the-tabarrok-curve-a-call-for-patent-reform-in-the-us/.

Gallagher, Dan. "Sonos Finally Hits the Hard Reset Button," *The Wall Street Journal*, February 9, 2025, https://www.wsj.com/tech/ sonos-finally-hits-the-hard-reset-button-bddde38f?siteid=yhoof2.

Goldman Sachs. "Global Financial Markets Crash on Black Monday." Goldman Sachs, accessed January 19, 2026. https://www.goldmansachs. com/our-firm/history/moments/1987-black-monday.

Greenspan, Alan. "The Challenge of Central Banking in a Democratic Society." Speech, Annual Dinner and Francis Boyer Lecture of The American Enterprise Institute for Public Policy Research (Washington, DC: December 5, 1996). https://www.federalreserve.gov/boarddocs/ speeches/1996/19961205.htm.

Quinn, Gene. "*Sonos v. Google*: A Decision Based on Ignorance of Patent Law That Must Be Overturned." IPWatchdog, November 2, 2023. https://ipwatchdog.com/2023/11/02/sonos-v-google-decision-based-ignorance-patent-law-must-overturned/id=169114/.

Sterne, Rob, and Gene Quinn. "Patent Death Squads: Are All Commercially Viable Patents Invalid?" IPWatchdog, March 24, 2014. https://ipwatchdog.com/2014/03/24/ptab-death-squads-are-all-commercially-viable-patents-invalid/id=48642/.

Tabarrok, Alex. "Patents, Intellectual Property and the Rise of the Rent Seeking Society." Marginal Revolution, September 27, 2023. https://marginalrevolution.com/marginalrevolution/2023/09/patents-intellectual-property-and-the-rise-of-the-rent-seeking-society.html.

U.S. Const., art. 1, §8, clause 8.

CHAPTER 2: THE IP PYRAMID FORTRESS

CIPU, "The Footprint of Patent History," IPBasics.org, accessed January 19, 2026, https://www.ipbasics.org/trends.

Cornell Law School. "35 U.S. Code § 316: Conduct of Inter Partes Review." (Preponderance of the Evidence Standard.) Legal Information Institute, accessed January 19, 2026. https://www.law.cornell.edu/uscode/text/35/316.

eBay Inc. v. MercExchange, LLC. 547 U.S. 388 (2006). https://supreme.justia.com/cases/federal/us/547/388/.

Heiden, Bowman. "How Large Patent Damages Awards Actually Play Out." Law360, December 3, 2025. https://www.law360.com/ip/articles/2416572?nl_pk=63a4c941-d47f-4b96-b43d-472749391804&utm_source=newsletter&utm_medium=email&utm_campaign=ip&utm_content=2025-12-04&read_main=1&nlsidx=0&nlaidx=13.

Jefferson, Thomas. Thomas Jefferson to Isaac McPherson, August 13, 1813. In *The Writings of Thomas Jefferson*, edited by Andrew A. Lipscomb and Albert Ellery Bergh, 13:333. Washington, DC: Thomas Jefferson Memorial Association, 1905.

Key, Madeleine. "Understanding IP Matters: Piracy or Policy? Maintaining U.S. Technology Leadership in the Digital Age." IPWatchdog, November 29, 2023. https://ipwatchdog.com/2023/11/29/understanding-ip-matters-piracy-policy-maintaining-u-s-technology-leadership-digital-age/.

Schreiner, Stephen, and Mitch Yang. "Perspectives on the PTAB's 70% All Claims Invalidation Rate." IPWatchdog, July 2, 2025. https://ipwatchdog.com/2025/07/02/perspectives-ptabs-70-claims-invalidation-rate/id=189971/.

StoneX. "What Is Arbitrage?" StoneX, accessed January 19, 2026. https://www.stonex.com/en/financial-glossary/arbitrage/.

Team Acadia. "Amazon Prime Day 2025: The Results." Acadia, July 15, 2025. https://acadia.io/amazon-prime-day-2025-the-results/.

USPTO. "2111 Claim Interpretation; Broadest Reasonable Interpretation [R-10.2019]." United States Patent and Trademark Office, accessed January 19, 2026. https://www.uspto.gov/web/offices/pac/mpep/s2111.html.

USPTO. *Intellectual Property and the U.S. Economy: Third Edition* (United States Patent and Trademark Office, 2022). https://www.uspto.gov/sites/default/files/documents/uspto-ip-us-economy-third-edition.pdf.

USPTO. "Patent Process Overview." United States Patent and Trademark Office, accessed January 19, 2026. https://www.uspto.gov/patents/basics/patent-process-overview.

Wex Definitions Team. "Patent Troll." Cornell Law School, Legal Information Institute, August 2020. https://www.law.cornell.edu/wex/patent_troll.

CHAPTER 3: THE PATENT WARS NEVER ENDED

Arndt, Andrea L. "Freedom to Operate Opinions: What Are They, and Why Are They Important?" Dickinson Wright, March 2022. https://www.dickinson-wright.com/news-alerts/arndt-freedom-to-operate-opinions.

Carlin, George. "George Carlin on Conspiracies." Jakenfavre, February 25, 2010. YouTube video, 0:48. https://youtu.be/VAFd4FdbJxs?si=FMEXSle5BdqWQLp8.

Duggan, Wayne. "Magnificent 7 Stocks: What Are They and How They Dominate the Market." *U.S. News & World Report*, November 3, 2025. https://money.usnews.com/investing/articles/magnificent-7-stocks-explainer.

EFF. "Stupid Patent of the Month." Electronic Frontier Foundation, accessed January 19, 2026. https://www.eff.org/issues/stupid-patent-month.

Foote, Keith D. "A Brief History of Cloud Computing." Dataversity, December 17, 2021. https://www.dataversity.net/brief-history-cloud-computing/.

Landua, Josh. "Cross-Licenses, Royalty Stacking, and Patent Disputes." Patent Progress, January 17, 2020. https://patentprogress.org/2020/01/cross-licenses-royalty-stacking-and-patent-disputes/.

LOT Network. Home page. Accessed January 19, 2026. https://lotnet.com/.

Myhrvold, Nathan. "Who We Are." Intellectual Ventures, accessed January 19, 2026. https://www.intellectualventures.com/who-we-are/leadership/nathan-myhrvold/.

Ott, Matt. "Lyft Shares Rocket 62% over a Typo in the Company's Earnings Release." AP News, last modified February 14, 2024. https://apnews.com/article/lyft-shares-earnings-typo-algorithm-6867a202e0017d75d3631edfb8a9ba15.

Park, Andrea. "Apple, Masimo Court Case over Smartwatch Trade Secrets Ends in Hung Jury." *Fierce Biotech*, May 3, 2023. https://www.fiercebiotech.com/medtech/apple-masimo-court-case-over-smartwatch-trade-secrets-ends-hung-jury.

Phelps, Marshall, and David Kline. *Burning the Ships: Transforming Your Company's Culture Through Intellectual Property Strategy*. Wiley, 2009.

Sable, Michael. "Understanding Corporate Venture Capital: The Ultimate Guide." *GoingVC*, October 27, 2022. https://www.goingvc.com/post/the-ultimate-guide-to-understanding-the-world-of-corporate-venture-capital.

Stanford Law School. "Mark A. Lemley: Biography." Stanford Law School, accessed January 19, 2026. https://law.stanford.edu/mark-a-lemley/.

UC Berkeley Law. "Colleen Chien: Profile." UC Berkeley Law, accessed January 19, 2026. https://www.law.berkeley.edu/our-faculty/faculty-profiles/colleen-chien/#tab_profile.

The University of Utah. "Jorge Contreras: Bio." The University of Utah, accessed January 19, 2026. https://profiles.faculty.utah.edu/u0989706.

WIPO. *Tool 5: Freedom to Operate*. WIPO, 2024. https://www.wipo.int/documents/d/tisc/docs-en-tisc-toolkit-freedom-to-operate-description.pdf.

CHAPTER 4: REDISCOVERING IP CAPITAL

Chien, Colleen V. "Holding Up and Holding Out." *Michigan Telecommunications and Technology Law Review* 21, no. 1 (2014). https://repository.law.umich.edu/mttlr/vol21/iss1/1/.

CoinGecko. "Cryptocurrency Prices by Market Cap." CoinGecko, accessed December 9, 2025. https://www.coingecko.com.

Damodaran, Aswath. "The Seven Samurai: How Big Tech Rescued the Market in 2023!" Musings on Markets (blog), February 8, 2024. https://aswathdamodaran.blogspot.com/2024/02/the-seven-samurai-how-big-tech-rescued.html.

Dodson, Drew, and Elizabeth Kettler. "Twenty Years of Sarbanes-Oxley Act: What Has SOX Achieved, and What's Next?" Stout, November 7, 2022. https://www.stout.com/en/insights/article/twenty-years-of-sarbanes-oxley-act-what-has-sox-achieved-whats-next.

Fonarev, Max. "Identifying Intangibles in Purchase Accounting." Sorbus Valuation Services, September 21, 2017. https://sorbusadvisors.com/identifying-intangibles-in-purchase-accounting.

Howarth, Josh. "Startup Failure Rate Statistics (2025)." Exploding Topics (blog), last modified June 5, 2025. https://explodingtopics.com/blog/startup-failure-stats.

Neufeld, Dorothy. "The $109 Trillion Global Stock Market in One Chart," Visual Capitalist, September 27, 2023. https://www.visualcapitalist.com/the-109-trillion-global-stock-market-in-one-chart.

Neufeld, Dorothy. "Global Debt Hits a New High of $315 Trillion." Visual Capitalist, August 13, 2024. https://www.visualcapitalist.com/global-debt-hits-a-new-high-of-315-trillion.

O'Hara, Nicole J. "David Bowie: Pioneer of Intellectual Property." *GrossMcGinley* (blog), January 15, 2016. https://www.grossmcginley.com/resources/blog/david-bowie-pioneer-of-intellectual-property/.

Park, Andrea. "Apple, Masimo Court Case over Smartwatch Trade Secretes Ends in Hung Jury." Fierce Biotech, May 3, 2023. https://www.fiercebiotech.com/medtech/apple-masimo-court-case-over-smartwatch-trade-secrets-ends-hung-jury.

RPX Empower (f/k/a RPX Insights). Home page. Last accessed December, 2023. https://insight.rpxcorp.com/

U.S. Securities and Exchange Commission, "Search Filings," accessed January 30, 2026, https://www.sec.gov/search-filings.,

Sudhindra, Nicole J. S. "Marvel's Superhero Licensing." *WIPO Magazine*, June 4, 2012. https://www.wipo.int/en/web/wipo-magazine/articles/marvels-superhero-licensing-38127.

Tavares, Ricardo. "The Rise of Algorithmic Trading: How AI Is Reshaping Financial Markets." *Forbes*, December 2, 2025. https://www.forbes.com/sites/delltechnologies/2025/12/02/the-rise-of-algorithmic-trading-how-ai-is-reshaping-financial-markets.

UN Trade and Development, *A World of Debt: Report 2025: It Is Time for Reform* (Geneva: United Nations Conference on Trade and Development, 2025). https://unctad.org/publication/world-of-debt.

CHAPTER 5: TIMING IS EVERYTHING

Bezos, Jeff. "405: Jeff Bezos: Amazon and Blue Origin." December 14, 2023. In *Lex Fridman Podcast*, 2:11:00, at 1:49:59. https://open.spotify.com/episode/5D4rToJ6IW2JsilsvuKeA1?si=0c2d3e93bfd44485.

Cengage. "Information About Our Restructuring." Cengage, accessed January 19, 2026. https://www.cengage.com/restructuring/.

Palmer, Will. "100 Percent Inspiration: GE Vernova's World-Changing Legacy of Innovation." GE, March 6, 2024. https://www.ge.com/news/taxonomy/term/400.

Petrou, Virginia. "What Happened to Nortel? The Rise and Fall of a Canadian Legend." *TXO* (blog), June 30, 2023. https://www.txo.com/resources/what-happened-to-nortel-the-rise-and-fall-of-a-canadian-legend/.

CHAPTER 6: DISRUPTING CREDIT CARDS

Revolution comes from independent inventors and evolution comes from large corporates. Baumol, William J. "Education for Innovation: Entrepreneurial Breakthroughs vs. Corporate Incremental Improvements." NBER, June 2004. https://www.nber.org/papers/w10578.

Chee, Foo Yun. "Apple to Face EU Antitrust Charge over NFC Chip: Sources." Reuters, October 6, 2021. https://www.reuters.com/technology/exclusive-eu-antitrust-regulators-charge-apple-over-its-nfc-chip-tech-sources-2021-10-06/.

Denso. "About the Patent." QRCode.com, accessed January 19, 2026. https://www.qrcode.com/en/patent.html.

Denso. "QR Codes Powering Digital Transformation—Inheriting the Inventor's Spirit of Innovation to Face the Next 30 Years." Driven Base, February 25, 2025. https://www.denso.com/global/en/driven-base/career-life/qr_engineer-1/.

SSO for Electronic Device Payments. The Federal Reserve, FedPayments Improvement. "Payments Landscape Series: Setting and Adopting Standards." Catalyst Corner, Payments Efficiency, accessed January 19, 2026. https://fedpaymentsimprovement.org/news/blog/payments-landscape-series-setting-and-adopting-standards/.

Johnston, Amber. "The Horrors of Doomscrolling and Its Impact on Mental Health." University of Colorado Denver, October 18, 2024. https://www.ucdenver.edu/student/stories/library/healthy-happy-life/the-horrors-of-doomscrolling-its-impact-on-mental-health.

Kats, Rimma. "Starbucks Aims to Increase Coffee Sales Via QR Code Campaign." Retail Dive, accessed January 19, 2026. https://www.retaildive.com/ex/mobilecommercedaily/starbucks-aims-to-increase-coffee-sales-via-qr-code-campaign.

Startups out-invent and innovate large companies. Start It Ventures. "The Innovation Paradox: How Small Startups Beat Big Corporates." *Stories: Corporate Venturing* (blog), January 30, 2025. https://startit-x.com/en/ventures/blog/how-small-startups-beat-big-corporates#:~:text=The%20answer%20lies%20in%20the,this%20potential%20is%20often%20wasted.

CHAPTER 7: INVESTOR HELL

CBS Mornings. "Widow of Theranos Scientist Blames Elizabeth Holmes for Her Husband's Death: 'She Has Shown No Remorse.'" *CBS News*, January 12, 2022. https://www.cbsnews.com/news/theranos-scientist-widow-elizabeth-holmes/.

Chernova, Yuliya. "More Startups Throw in the Towel, Unable to Raise Money for Their Ideas." *The Wall Street Journal*, June 9, 2023. https://www.wsj.com/articles/more-startups-throw-in-the-towel-unable-to-raise-money-for-their-ideas-eff8305b?st=RyANP3.

McKenna, Francine. "Theranos Closes Deal with Fortress to Shut Down Embattled Firm." *The Wall Street Journal*, September 14, 2018. https://www.wsj.com/articles/theranos-closes-deal-with-fortress-to-shut-down-embattled-firm-1536932154.

Mersino, Paul, and Jennifer Dukarski. "Waymo v. Uber: 'Epic' Trade Secret Case Involving Autonomous Vehicles Settles for $244 Million." Butzel Attorneys and Counselors, news release, February 12, 2018. https://www.butzel.com/alert-Waymo-v-Uber-Epic-Trade-Secret-Case-Involving-Autonomous-Vehicles-Settles-for-244-Million.

Percival, Shane. "Fortress Investment Group: Bad Actor, Bad Timing, or Both?" Nod Law, June 24, 2020. https://www.nod-law.com/fortress-investment-group/.

Fortress offers patents royalty-free for COVID. Quinn, Gene. "Twisting Facts to Capitalize on COVID-19 Tragedy: Fortress v. bioMerieux." IPWatchdog, March 18, 2020. https://ipwatchdog.com/2020/03/18/twisting-facts-capitalize-covid-19-tragedy-fortress-v-biomerieux/id=119941/.

Rosenbush, Stephen. "'Scaling Through Chaos': How the World's Fastest-Growing Startups Get That Way." *The Wall Street Journal*, October 31, 2024. https://www.wsj.com/articles/scaling-through-chaos-how-the-worlds-fastest-growing-startups-get-that-way-efc398d3?st=NZRP3p.

Schultz, Mark. *The Importance of an Effective and Reliable Patent System to Investment in Critical Technologies.* University of Akron School of Law, 2022. https://cip2.gmu.edu/wp-content/uploads/sites/31/2022/09/Panel-4-Mark-Schultz-VC-Funding-IPW.pdf.

Starboard Value LP, "Starboard Files Investor Presentation and Sends Letter to AOL Shareholders," *PR Newswire*, May 7, 2012, https://www.prnewswire.com/news-releases/starboard-files-investor-presentation-and-sends-letter-to-aol-shareholders-150449795.html.

Terry, Mark. "Theranos Avoids Bankruptcy by Snagging a $100M Lifeline from Fortress." BioSpace, December 27, 2017. https://www.biospace.com/unique-theranos-avoids-bankruptcy-by-snagging-a-100m-lifeline-from-fortress.

VC firms invest less in patent-intensive industries. USIJ. "USIJ Releases Report on the Importance of an Effective and Reliable Patent System to Critical Technologies." USIJ, news release, August 3, 2020. https://usij.org/usij-releases-report-on-the-importance-of-an-effective-and-reliable-patent-system-to-critical-technologies/.

CHAPTER 8: EVOLVING PATENT STRATEGIES

Arndt, Andrea L. "Freedom to Operate Opinions: What Are They, and Why Are They Important?" Dickinson Wright, March 2022, https://www.dickinson-wright.com/news-alerts/arndt-freedom-to-operate-opinions.

Colchester, Max. "The Irish Government Is Unbelievably Rich. It's Largely Thanks to Uncle Sam." *The Wall Street Journal*, last modified November 22, 2024. https://www.wsj.com/world/europe/the-irish-government-is-unbelievably-rich-its-largely-thanks-to-uncle-sam-92494310.

Eden, Lorraine. "Lorraine Eden's Publications on Transfer Pricing, International Tax and Public Finance." Vox Professori, last modified April 14, 2025. https://www.voxprof.com/eden/eden-publications-tp-tax.html.

IPDefine. Home page. Accessed January 19, 2026. https://ipdefine.com/.

Kiel, Paul. "The IRS Decided to Get Tough Against Microsoft. Microsoft Got Tougher." ProPublica, January 22, 2020. https://www.propublica.org/article/the-irs-decided-to-get-tough-against-microsoft-microsoft-got-tougher.

Lee, Ricki. "EU Strikes a Blow Against Apple and Google in Landmark Rulings." Tech Informed, September 11, 2024. https://techinformed.com/eu-rulings-apple-google-antitrust-taxes/.

Mims, Christopher. "The Main Driver of Apple's Success
Has Become Its Biggest Liability." *The Wall Street Journal*,
January 26, 2024. https://www.wsj.com/tech/personal-tech/
apple-vision-pro-walled-garden-mac-iphone-app-store-c4838278.

Morris, Angela. "IPwe's Bankruptcy Takes a Turn for the Worse."
IAM, March 26, 2024. https://www.iam-media.com/article/
ipwes-bankruptcy-takes-turn-the-worse.

Setser, Brad W. "The Spotty International Tax Record
of Big U.S. Technology Companies." Council on Foreign
Relations, July 28, 2024. https://www.cfr.org/blog/
spotty-international-tax-record-big-us-technology-companies.

Steele, Merritt L. "The Great Failure of the IPXI Experiment: Why
Commoditization of Intellectual Property Failed." *Cornell Law Review* 102,
no. 4 (May 2017). https://scholarship.law.cornell.edu/clr/vol102/iss4/5/.

CHAPTER 9: THE DOUBLE-EDGED
SWORD OF PATENT ATTORNEYS

Aspen, Michelle, and Jonathan Stroud. "Fire First, Ask Questions Later:
The New Normal of No-Notice Patent Suits." *JUVE Patent*, September
24, 2024. https://www.juve-patent.com/sponsored/unified-patents-llc/
fire-first-ask-questions-later-the-new-normal-of-no-notice-patent-suits/.

Heath, "Eric Schmidt Says the Quiet Part Out Loud," *The Verge*,
August 16, 2024, https://www.theverge.com/2024/8/16/24221353/
eric-schmidt-says-the-quiet-part-out-loud.

Quinn, Renee C. "Google Announces the Patent Purchase Promotion
to Foster Innovation." IPWatchdog, April 29, 2015. https://ipwatchdog.
com/2015/04/29/google-announces-the-patent-purchase-promotion/.

Schmidt, Eric. "The Age of AI." Transcript, Stanford, 2024.
https://github.com/ociubotaru/transcripts/blob/main/
Stanford_ECON295%E2%A7%B8CS323_I_2024_I_The_Age_of_AI%2C_
Eric_Schmidt.txt.

CHAPTER 10: THE GOVERNMENT'S ROLE IN FIXING PATENTS

Barnett, Jonathan M. *The Big Steal: Ideology, Interest, and the Undoing of Intellectual Property.* Oxford University Press, 2024, Introduction, p 6.

Graham, Paul. "Defining Property." Paul Graham (blog), March 2012. https://paulgraham.com/property.html.

USPTO. "Patent Pro Bono Program: Free Patent Legal Assistance." United States Patent and Trademark Office. https://www.uspto.gov/patents/basics/using-legal-services/pro-bono/patent-pro-bono-program.

CHAPTER 11: REBUILD THE SYSTEM

Bensussan, Hannah, and Cédric Durand. "Hundred Years of Corporate Planning. From Industrial Capitalism to Intellectual Monopoly Capitalism Through the Lenses of the *Harvard Business Review* (1922–2021)." *Socio-Economic Review,* Oxford University Press, 2025. https://s100.copyright.com/AppDispatchServlet?publisherName=OUP&publication=1475-147X&title.

Houlihan Lokey. "Purchase Price Allocation Study." Houlihan Lokey, accessed January 21, 2026. https://hl.com/insights/purchase-price-allocation-study/.

Khullar, Arshiya, ed. "The Next Era of Private Credit." McKinsey & Company, September 24, 2024. https://www.mckinsey.com/industries/private-capital/our-insights/the-next-era-of-private-credit.

Tilley, Aaron, and Dean Seal. "Apple Earmarks $500 Billion for U.S. Expansion." *The Wall Street Journal,* last modified February 24, 2025. https://www.wsj.com/tech/apple-500-billion-investment-us-19ca11a0?st=dLCQMH.

United States Patent and Trademark Office. "Patent Pro Bono Program: Free Patent Legal Assistance." Accessed November 17, 2025. https://www.uspto.gov/patents/basics/using-legal-services/pro-bono/patent-pro-bono-program.

US Department of Commerce. "U.S. Patent and Trademark Office" and "Leadership." US Department of Commerce, accessed January 21, 2026. https://www.commerce.gov/bureaus-and-offices/uspto.

USDOT, "Part I: History," US Department of Transportation Federal Highway Administration, accessed January 21, 2026, https://highways.dot.gov/highway-history/interstate-system/ dwight-d-eisenhower-system-interstate-and-defense-highways/part-i.

USPTO. "Intellectual Property and the U.S. Economy: Third Edition." United States Patent and Trademark Office, 2022, accessed January 21, 2026. https://www.uspto.gov/ip-policy/economic-research/ intellectual-property-and-us-economy.

CHAPTER 12: BUILDING AND PAYING FOR THE NEW PATENT SYSTEM

Brown, Annie, Annabella Garnham, Anmol Kaur Grewal, Lorena Rivera Leon, and Sacha Wunsch-Vincent. "The Value of Intangible Assets of Corporations Worldwide Rebounds to All-Time High of USD 80 Trillion in 2024." WIPO, February 28, 2025. https:// www.wipo.int/en/web/global-innovation-index/w/blogs/2025/ the-value-of-intangible-assets-of-corporations.

www.ingramcontent.com/pod-product-compliance
Lightning Source LLC
Chambersburg PA
CBHW032004050726

47590CB00006B/2036